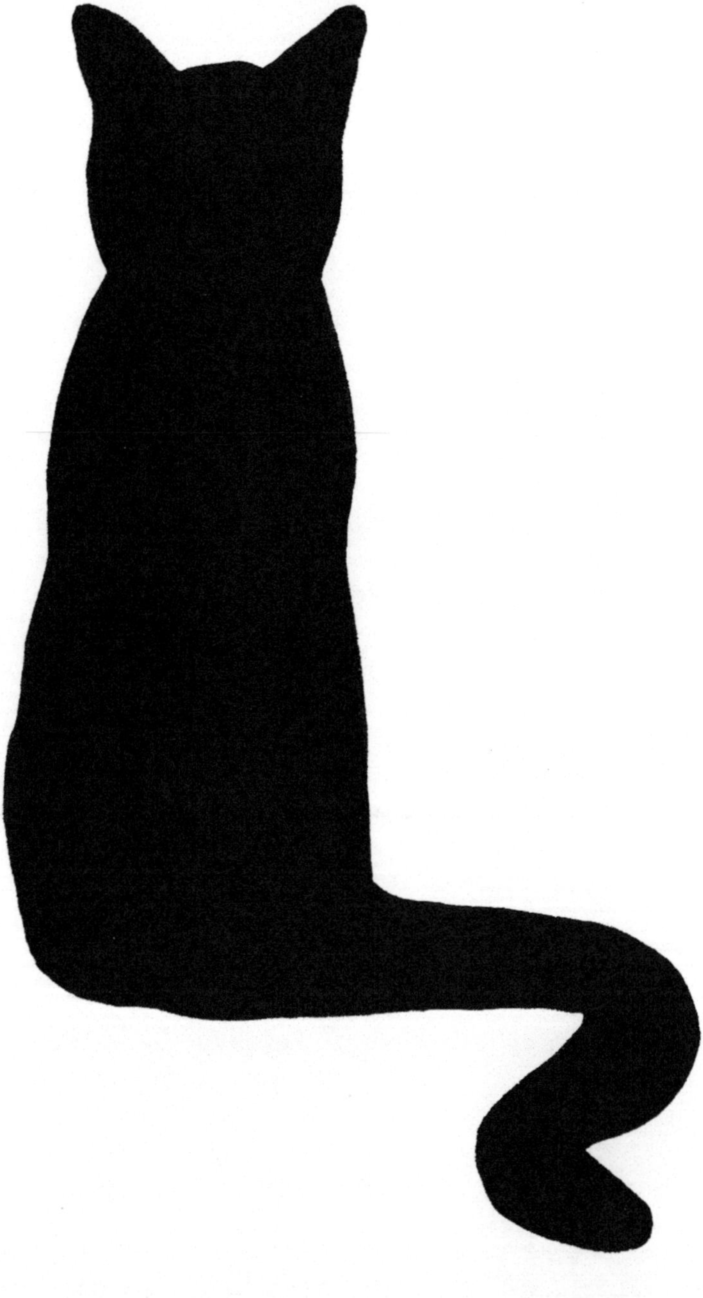

Words by Jacob Davies.

Edit and design by Jacob Davies.

Illustrations by Abi Cryer.

Cover photo by Olga Kaya.

Author image by Peter Richardson.

Back cover photo by Paul Davies.

All other images by Jacob Davies, unless credited otherwise.

Printed by Book Printing UK
Remus House, Coltsfoot Drive, Peterborough, PE2 9BF

Printed in Great Britain

ISBN: 978-1-3999-2097-1

ALSO BY THE AUTHOR...

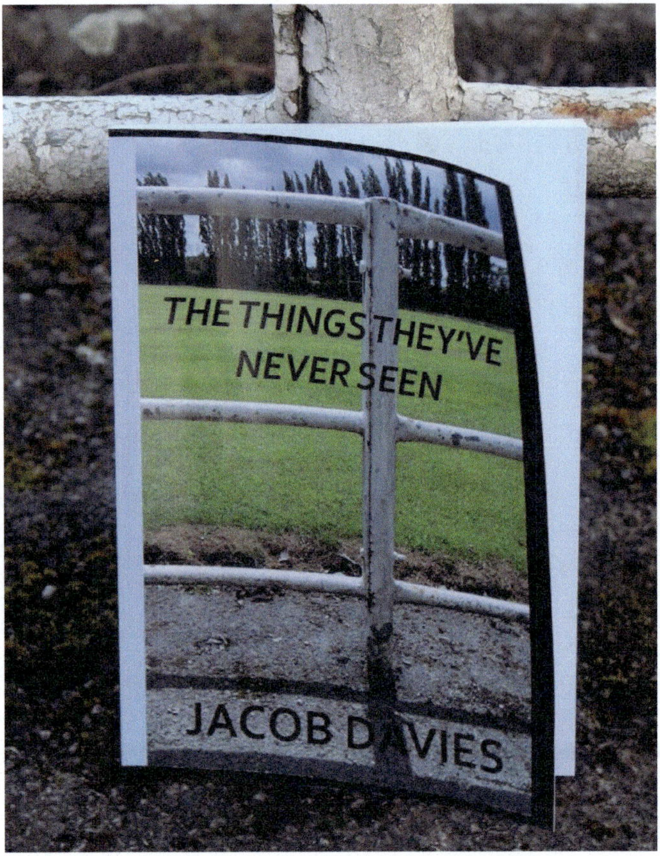

'THE THINGS THEY'VE NEVER SEEN'

– DECEMBER 2020

CONTENTS

SECTION A

CONTENTS

SECTION B

“Although our conversation be, as wordless as the windy sky”

John Betjeman

‘EVERY NIGHT IS NOVEMBER’

JACOB DAVIES

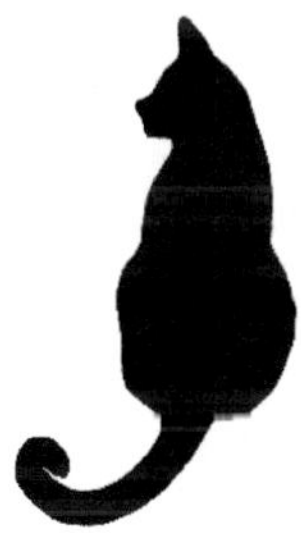

INTRODUCTION – WHAT IS NOVEMBER?

November has an unmistakable, unavoidable presence and stature.
November is graceful, delicate and gentle.
November is sharp and alluringly defiant.
November is streetlights above, beaming down golden flashes, onto dull and dreary rain-embraced English pavements.
November is *'I didn't'*.
November demands attention, dragging the eyes of the awestruck towards it.
November is fixating on the spellbinding beauty of the night.
November is captivating, as much in the way it stops, as in the way it moves.
November is golden flashes of exquisiteness.
November is a lachrymose electricity.
November is moonlight.
November is silence.
November is art.
November is Alister and Gemini.
November is *'Like Dylan in the Movies'*
November is the bassline.
November is gothic.
November is a dripping, wax-wilting candle lit flame; hunched back, fighting with the resistance of a gale force wind.
November is '*Wayward Sisters'*.
November will appear.

November is a voice to be lost in, spinning in the richness of raw honestly and brutality.
November is a dream of a slanted rooftop, gazing upwards on a smog-coated night.
November drags towards the stars.
November is your hair, fresh out of the rain.
November is your charming imperfections.
November is a dream to drag along, through the grey and mundane days.
November is the words of your soul, tinged and dusted with irony and gallows humour.
November is a roaring, colourful picture of a happy delusion.
November is morally and creatively bankrupt.
November exists in memoriam of all that is lost, all that is being lost, and all that is yet to be lost.
November is a cenotaph, a decorated memorial of such dread.
November nights are the sun and the moon sharing the same sky.
November is reaching for a door handle in pitch black darkness.
November is resignation.
November is caused by wintery days that go on for just an hour too long.
November is the imagined, the unimaginable, the untouchable and the real.
November is *'The Girl from Tel-Aviv who Wouldn't Kneel'*.
November is a stone-cold face but delicate soul.
November is the quick and quiet evaporation of months of unity, the dissipation of years of understanding and the collapse of decades of strength.
November is those who have departed this journey.

November is the death of loyalty.
November is losing summer days that have passed by.
November is when nightfall approaches, and lights go out.
November is the end of the world, the end of the road.
November is when the machine stops.
November is an explosion of darkness.
November is your open soul on the streets.

November is streetlights, inquisitively gazing into the mind
November is the hope drained from mankind
November is the point I still must prove
November is what remains of me and you
November is all that is bereft
November is all that is left
Beware the month, that starts and ends with a one.

Every night is November; you must be trapped here, or at least
Have the rips on your skin to remember
That I have nothing further to give, November has won.
Truly, every night is November.
Every night is November.

These words are the prisms of peril
That stitch November together.
These words are the stomach lining of dusk laden dread
To sit with you forever.
These words are all I have given
And the little I have left.
These words are the things I have seen
The things we have seen.
These words are what is to follow...

Every night is November; you must be trapped here, or at least
Have the rips on your skin to remember
That I have nothing further to give, November has won.
Truly, every night is November.
Every night is November.

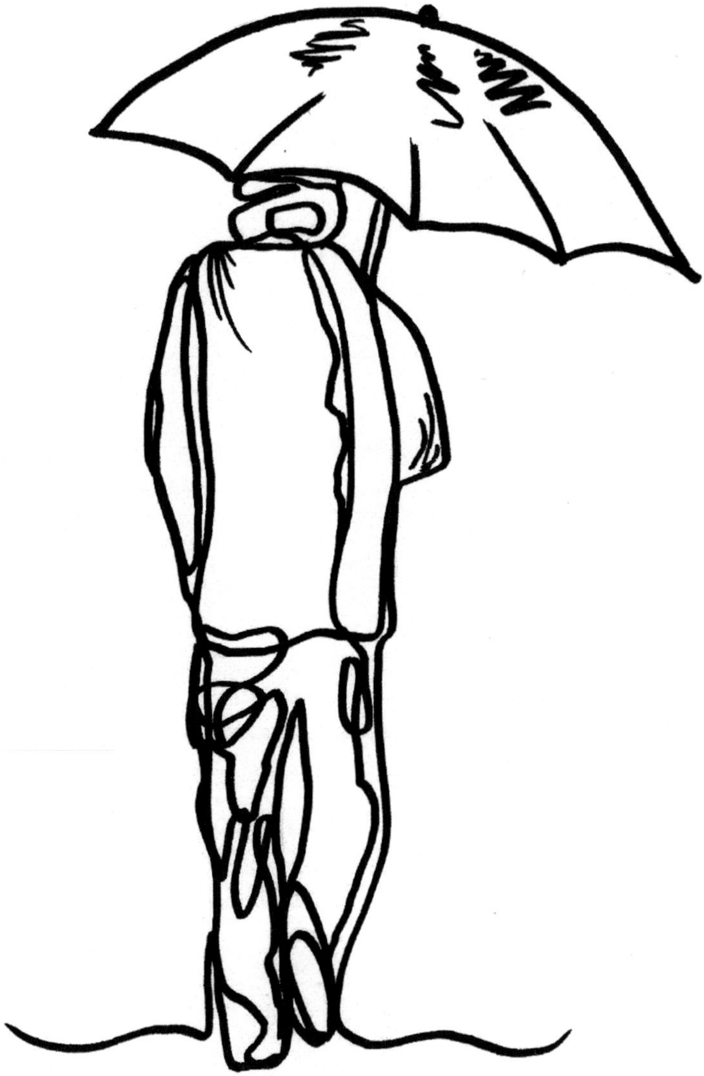

SECTION A

THE MORNING CAME, AND EVERYONE WAS GONE

He spent the night
Painting the local home for the old aged, a lovely shade of beige
You can never tell
Where happiness will come from
But morning came, and everyone was gone

Reflecting from the patio door
He gazes into the fire, as he did as a child
No longer warm flickering flames, the hope he saw before
He sees a burning hot fate
So very mundane, dizzying and wild

Marvellously miserable Monday
Waking without the tinge of tear-coated frost
Or single afternoon starved of a lion's roar of thunder
Was out of the question since day one
Nevertheless, the morning came, and everyone was gone

Miserably marvellous Monday
Lies with grit and might, soon to be thrown and forgotten
His feeble body, dragged and wrestled
Pulled by gravity, to rock bottom

He knows how
He has fallen to his knees
And how he has cried
Before
But surely, this is the last time

He looked out of the window

And there, plain to see
Was their absence, standing there
All around, with waving arms, upright and determinedly

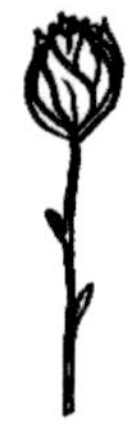

Blinding, crashing flashbacks
Falling into a delusional state
All utterly meaningless now
As his heart began to split, bend and break
The morning came, and everyone was gone

He knows how
He drowned in his sorrows
And died
Many times,
This is just the first time
The more you flail in the water, the quicker you drown

They'll all come back
With smiles chiselled into their chiselled faces
With lovely stories to tell
About more interesting people, and nicer places

They'll all come back
With memories, beyond compare
The stories they'll tell
It will be almost as if, he was there

They'll all come back
With their horizons broadened
Until then, he is left to rue each of his mistakes
With Herbert Khaury and W.H. Auden.

His heart raced, sank and was discarded in a moment
With each sheepish smile and half-withdrawn goodbye
Leaving the past behind

Where savage smiles were cast, and he flew high

"I am held down, and held back", she said
She told him, as she looked him half in the face
He rushed home and searched hard, to find
His very last cling-able happy place
The morning came, and everyone was gone

Every night is November
Familiar, sorrowful chime
As her gaze drifted away
He knew it'd be the last time
He knew what had come, would come
He woke in the morning
And everyone was gone

Nothing good has ever come
From saying the same thing twice
Polyamorous, means one isn't good enough
Thus, a life above cracking ice

Nothing fun has ever sprung
From staying up all night
Polyamorous, means he isn't good enough
Hope becomes a boat, drifting further out of sight

Nothing
Nothing
Nothing can be done
To make any of this alright

Every night is November
Oh, so familiar, sorrowful chime
As her gaze drifted away
He knew it'd be the last time

He always knew this day would come
He woke in the morning
And everyone was gone

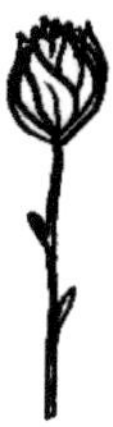

"The birdsong at 2am, and news which cannot be shared
Serves as the alarm call that I am all alone
As they leave, those who once were behind me
Move away to live in broken promises, and snapped lines of the telephone

With the frightened sun
Glaring in troubled warmth on my head
Lay here, aside my solitude
Clear and open wide
The words I never said
The morning came, and everyone was gone

I know how
I've followed you around
I've smiled,
Many times,
But you know all my reasons why
I cannot smile anymore.
I cannot follow you, anymore.

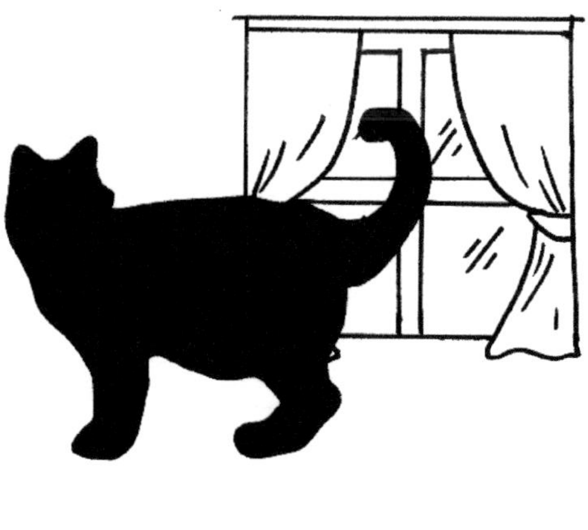

Whispers. In a bottle
Whispers. When the night is dark
Spiders. Roam the room
Spiders. When the night is dark

They'll all come back
With lovely hair!
The stories they'll tell,
It will be almost as if, I was there
It will be almost as if
I am here.
Almost as if
Absolutely lovely hair!

Lies. Cheap and easily spouted.
Lies. When the night is dark.
Alone. Comes around often.
Alone. When the night is dark.

He woke in the morning
And everyone was gone
He woke in the morning
And everyone was gone
He woke in the
Everyone
And everyone was
Mourning

He woke in the morning
And everyone was gone

Whispers
Spiders
Whispers
Spiders

Lies
Alone
Lies
Alone"

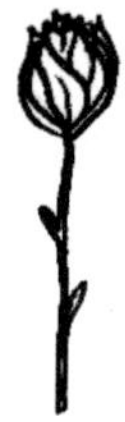

Every night is November
This is such a familiar, sorrowful chime
Her gaze drifted away
He knew it'd be the last time
His heart knew
It would be the last time

HENRY'S HANDS

Bitter sands dust the sky-pointing rooftops
Of bitterly cold mountains
Henry's hands lay bare, and tinged with reds and greys
Dearly departed, for many days.

Henry's hands remember all the pain
Lay bitten by frost,
Frozen in the moment
Where the cold cut them off.

Henry's hands are swept away by the ocean
With the man-made land,
Dishevelled near the pebbles
Yet the worst to come, has not been planned.

Henry's hands are a snapshot of a dreadful night
A reminder in the morning of what you did,
I'm sure it seems tempting, though it is useless
To hide behind your eyelids.

Henry knows the extent of the woes
He causes and he creates
A place for your delusions to break
And your shattering earth to shake.

And see now how, he's lost everything
Yet has every new pain to gain
Henry's hands, they tease and play
The source of impenetrable drivel, locked away.

Henry's hands
Lay torn on deforested land

In binary, or in worn finery
Henry's hands bring no refuge to the damned.

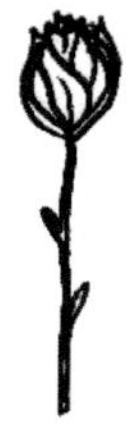

Henry's hands, break with venomous screams
From the captive cocoon
Fingernails snap in wretched dreams
On the lid of his tomb.

Bitter sands are swept away
Dearly departed, for many days
Henry's hands are open and bare
Never a gift to give, nor spare.

Henry's hands spread the disease of lingering broken hearts
Henry's hands drew them apart
They live in the nauseating middle ground
Controlling the busy people, you've seen around
Henry's hands are yours, in a flaming, fiery glove.
At any one moment
The many mannerisms, and the love
Must stop.

I'M ALMOST CERTAIN SUMMER WILL COME

Half a second from heaven,
The soft buzz, late spring night
Kisses your forehead, perplexing rest
Just gently
Brushing your fingertips with dread

Very nearly heaven
This hazy, lazy middle ground
Confusion of the air to be cold
Or to be warm.
And you rest there,
Transfixed, stationary
The dexterity of the day,
Sits with your disquiets.
Just softly,
As you wander away.

So, smile just for a moment,
Remember it shall not last.
Let your shoulders drop
With me
Be utterly soothed
By such an overcast.
I'm almost certain,
Summer will come again.

As gentle and tender,
As the caress of the solstice
Wave, softly goodbye
To each stress of a life

The dark summer days
Are waiting
Just waiting
They're waiting, to take you
Away.

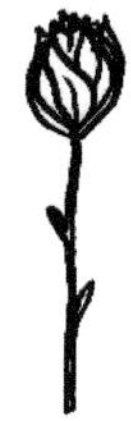

So, you whisper, quite slowly,
"How could I feel any more alone?"
Those feelings are real
They are true, though
You are never too far
From lost ones
Summer's evil eyes, brings ever closer
Each year
Those who have been taken
Taken
Away.

The look of steady intent,
In suffering eyes
Gently mesmerised
By your nervous cries.
Those secluded brown eyes
Will always be watching
Watching
When you drift
Away
From awake.

A gentle breeze
Over from where they live
You shall live with them soon
Stumble towards that wall
Towards
Where they lay

Slowly, your tears,
Shall disappear away.

So, know I'll always love you
As we amble on our way
Long, long, long road home
Blackbird fly
As we amble on our way
Long, long road home
To cry, smile or die
As we amble like
Two loose kites drifting
Across the sky
As we amble towards
The ones you lost to the stars
They return
Return
To sit beside you
And to smile, today.

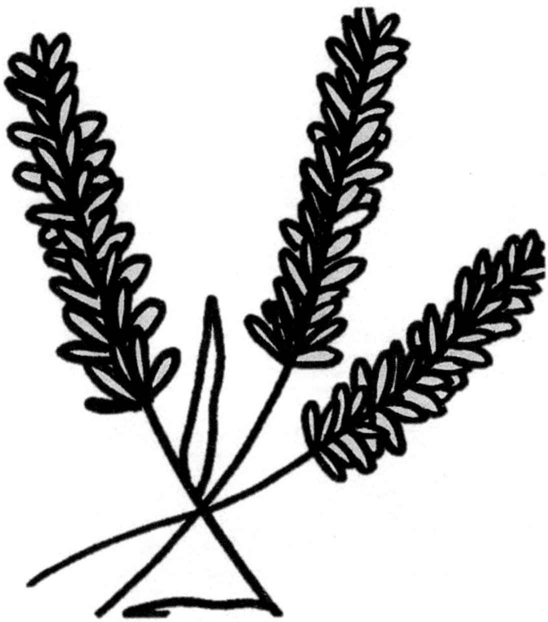

Every day
History plays
The same midnight chimes
I may not make it out alive this time
The bright summer sunshine
Lays with you, it lays
As you rest
And as life slips away.

Look at what's around you,
Summer sun bleeds towards
Your bleeding, drifting body
I am sure
Surer than I have ever been before…

I am sure.
Look in my eyes.
See into my heart.
I am sure, so sure.
So, so, so, so sure…

But look at what's around you
They all gather to mourn you
I'm certain
Almost certain
Summer will come again.

LET THE BOY DREAM

That little glance of screaming anguish
Turns into a small, silent tear
As in a second pass, the passing years
Never to be brought back.
Youth tells us that a grin solves all
The structure of home, familiarity adored,
The guiding supervisory skirting boards
Of hopeless courage.
We know deep down, hurt is birthed in youth,
Let the boy dream, before he knows the truth.

Childhood is all wrong,
Each day a new dream gone
No fun left to be had
Anymore.
To cry and cry all day, because of the loss
Of a plastic symbol of freedom, of fun with no cost
Of who could never bring anything but joy
A friend.
Is the first step to know the ways,
Of the sadness laid out, for the rest of your days.

The brittle tremble of what you cannot ever have back
The incomprehensible grief of this
Left in the lonely abyss -
Sheer hurt.
In the heart of a child
Who only wants to smile
Let the boy dream
Please.
The face of the frightened; alone and unloved
A visage that drops so low; fears born and summoned

Heartbreak in the young
Is common, yet so very raw
Ripped to shreds, what is adored
The lonely child.
Because nothing in the world matters more
How could anything matter more?
Than a sense of hope?
Completely torn.
Let the boy dream!
The least he deserves, is the chance to believe.

A light balloon, the shape of a train
Floats out of view, and far away
Every day I still feel this pain.
Let the boy dream
Before the emerging darkness of what's bereft
Because one of these days
The dreams are all he'll have left.

WHAT I SEE IN DARK NIGHTS

My thoughts and orations are
Welcomed by the streets
What I see in dark nights
Is a reason to be alive.

Mixed with wind and rain and shame
An element of anticipation
What I see in dark nights
Is a reason to be alive.

My soul cries exclamations, and begs for an explanation
Of past summer mornings, winter evenings
What I see in dark nights
Is an answer as to why.

The smell of smoke brings
November, September, never!
What I see in dark nights
An answer as to why.

Love has sped out the door
The 21st century has no need for it, anymore
What I see in dark nights
A place to miss saying goodbye.

I am becoming a shadow
Perhaps I died - with you
A few months ago?

Despite how much
You know I have tried
To cling on to what has gone

Memories, they fossilise.

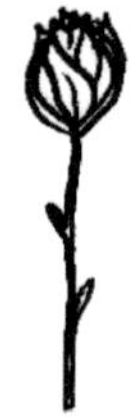

I am becoming a shadow
Perhaps I died, with you
A few months ago?

Have you ever felt an evening so still?
A subsiding of the sun so utterly tranquil?
The light splatters across my face
Gently, as it smashes the disgrace
Of Yorkshire houses, grotesque and tall
It smashes with ease the crumbling walls
An aura of dismay around
Enters my body through this merciless ground
The caress of delicate light
In such deserted night
Is for now, just enough
Just enough.
The resting of easy light
Soul lighting night
The comfort!
Always, my friend, I am a child
Subordinate to the night, I am mild.
A slanted roof
Tips out of reach, my youth
Anxiety trapped within
Dread built in the atoms of my skin
To sense the next spark,
To stand in the dark
Is to see each passing year
As they motionlessly, disappear
To feel a sensory spark,
To stand in the dark
Is to perform to your fears
To acknowledge your tears

Of both the past
How long will they last?
And the many future days
Now going astray
Whether the weather is night or dawn
What I gladly mourn
Will always return
Never, ever adjourn
There is no escape
It will return
It will never adjourn
Silent and afraid, in the arms of each night

I am becoming a shadow
Perhaps I died - with you
A few months ago.

DEARESTa

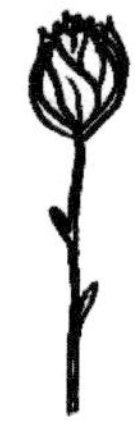

Dearest, I have news for you
Prepare yourself, it is not the best
We must make the most
Of the little time we have left.

Please know when I am gone
The science of love, the science of loss
Neither can be measured
In your arms I found somewhere to belong
I felt truly treasured.

Walk through the lake
The gentle, water stream
That is where I will be
When I can no longer look at you
I shall carry you around
In the background
Who knew, I was this early in the queue?
Please take comfort when we are no longer
To leave this hurricane behind
I shall be so much stronger
Dearest, I will be free to rest with the moon.

This isn't my first visit
To this hazy planet
For I pack with me in my bag, each ill and each woe
I am the child of wherever it is I am next to go.

Whilst I am here, I can half your fear and worry
For just a few final months I can delay eternal wrong
But dearest, I'm afraid we must hurry
For I haven't got long.

LIFE IN THE BUS LANE

Greeted by pitiful engine roars
And eyes that flickered, and were held bored
Almost like company, in their unpredictably
How long can dread be ignored?
How his poor mother must have cried
To see the dripping blood on his wrists, now dried
And no look of life
Left in his open eyes.

After my own tailor-made assassination
By societal socialisation,
I'm going somewhere much nicer now
Clunky wheels, always pointing in the wrong direction
Propel around this town, in daytime
Closing my eyes
As if that makes the truth
Less true.

Sat amidst chipped light blue paint, diluted with bacteria
A throbbingly disappointing single decker, under dispirited sky
What a wonderful way
To say goodbye

Put yourself in the shoes of your own childhood
And stare down at the disappointed face, that unfortunately looks like yours
Maybe you can then take some comfort, in losing another day
How long can what's real, be ignored?
How what's inside me resists and cries
Taking to rolling pavement, passing sorrow as we drive
This is life in the bus lane
The reflection of gloom in my eyes

I'll see you in a week
If I don't lose my newly gained, ingrained docility
And smash my head on the sink,
Which, is a very real possibility.

Sat amidst chipped light blue paint, diluted with bacteria
A throbbingly disappointing single decker, under dispirited sky
What a wonderful way
To say goodbye.

BOMB SHELTER

If a nuclear bomb
Was about to hit,
I'd build a bomb shelter
For my guinea pigs

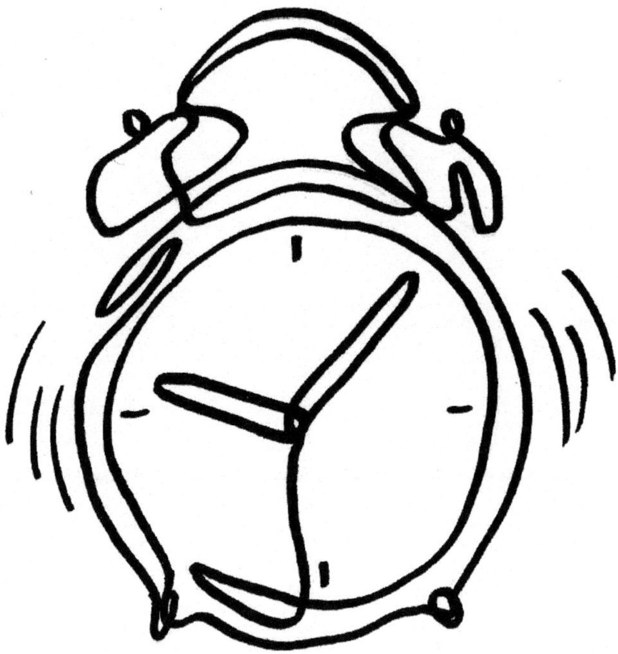

DON'T SURRENDER, DOROTHY

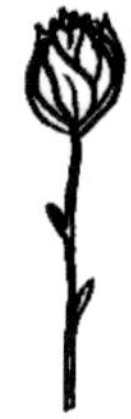

I have fallen so deeply in love with your gentle philosophy
The tremendous tone of truth, from under the floorboards
Don't surrender, Dorothy

The most marvellous member of our melancholic minority
Sharing a *'Monster'*, we both recognise and walk towards
I have fallen so deeply in love with your gentle philosophy

'Build a Problem', break a heart, bring a smile momentarily
Turn an elusive, subtle soul to wraithlike, rough records
Don't surrender, Dorothy

How your soft voice rings out such familiarity
Though I know you belong to someone else, and I am not yours
I have fallen so deeply in love with your gentle philosophy

I found you; finally, one in the world to whisper my sincerity
There is so much pain hidden between echoing chords
Don't surrender, Dorothy

You have sparked such unspeakable curiosity
You are the soundtrack to all I have lost, and can no longer afford
I have fallen so deeply in love with your gentle philosophy
So, please don't surrender, Dorothy
Don't you dare ever surrender, Dorothy.

THE PEOPLE I SEE IN MY DREAMS PT.1

The people I see in my dreams
Please don't take them away from me
Why do you need more from me?
You have my arms, my legs, my skin, my face
You have already taken all of my days

The people I see in my dreams
Don't pack them away, to hell, or to gaol
Or to university.
They must stay here with me.

The people that live in my dreams
No, don't take them away from me
What more could you need from me?
You have stripped those who tip-toed
Through the tulips with me

Why is it so much harder to confess wholehearted actualities
When you know you really mean them?
Why does the truth make you retch?
As soon as you stand up and speak it?
The people I see in my dreams
You're going to take them away from me.

I have seen far too many scenes
To lose, the people I see in my dreams
Don't tear both my life and fantasies in half
I have had and lost more than they'll ever have
I found and felt each strike of the belt
With this hand I have been dealt

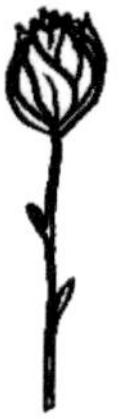

I am here, waving in towering cries
Whenever the sun next decides to rise
The people I see in my dreams

I am here, trying very hard not to give up
Whenever the sun next decides to rise
The people I see in my dreams

Please God, don't steal them from my arms.

MY ONLY FRIEND

I don't know if you'll remember
Though probably not.
A long while ago now, we lived in a world
One that since has been lost.

Delight was served on wooden menus
As the crowds smiled and cheered;
For an hour or two to set aside our woes
From the quickly passing years. And there they went.

I used to lay awake at night and worry like hell
What would happen if you weren't alive?
Never once did it cross my fledgling, juvenile mind
That I would be the one to die. And there I went.

I still can hear collective laughter
Echo slowly with the cars on the street, as they pass
Please, just give me one more day
Let me have a few more hours, let me go back. I can't.

How did I grow old so quick?
The unescapable loneliness makes me sick
Always the strongest pain, for what is impossible to retrieve
Yesterday's rain has fled, it is so hard to believe. I can't believe.

In the evening now, all I have is my tears
As I hear that music again
One day came around, where I was too old
I had lost my only friend.

WHEN AUGUST KNOWS WHO I AM

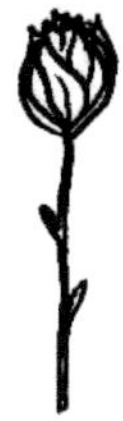

When August knows who I am,
For just a few short days,
It's quite easy to forget
Life was any other way.

When August grass sparks scents of memories behind
And knows my name
Instantly light, free and naive
I am skippingly alive; capering again.

When August cars pass by, in sixty-three
Different colours, know my thoughts
Never could calm contentment and restfulness
Be given away lightly, or sold short.

When August air drifts through the window,
And embraces my lungs
I know the heart is free
Sadness is done.

AUDREY

On her day of mourning,
There'll be no time for afternoon tea.
On the weekend we remember her life
(Thank God)
There'll be no more tears and no more toast,
Audrey I'm sure knows what is to follow
For her pain is in the post.

The world didn't know it was possible
To see a smile
With so little love, held inside
Those rose-petalled lips of time-frozen eternity
All sense of structure in God's earth, now gone
Her face, such enchanting eyes
Stared this gift horse in the mouth, and come out alive
Mankind only has once
She lives to give her most sparking looks
To anyone but you.

Audrey is tastelessly superglued to a pedestal,
It sickens many folks
That she is the vision of home.
Not a single soul can decide,
If this planet's biggest pain and fear
Is the torment that she is still here,
Or the reality that she is not.

Tell her, the queen of arts!
How falling deeply in love with circumstance
Isn't really love at all
To try to understand
The contradiction of her actions

And her words
Would be somewhat of a miscue
Audrey only believes the words
That she wishes to be true.

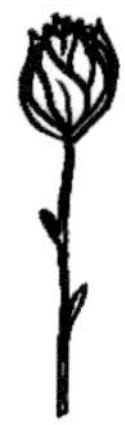

I once endured a night
Where I saw a piece of her heart
Whilst in came impeding autumnal dread
And whispers of a new start
Ambled timidly into view
That day will stay
As the last time I saw you
I still hear the laughter
The silence
The cries for more
Many days after a story
Performed years before

All those delicate tracks clocked in
At just over a minute
Scribbling, screaming and hurriedly today
I can taste those otherworldly tunes
They say clearly how - too much time has passed
To heal old, gaping wounds
If you ever see me again
Will you tell me all the stories,
You've heard about them?

I sit on summer evenings
And hear light bird song
Trapping my soul in chaotic yesterdays
Yesterday, it was
The raucous sound I held so close, and instantly knew
Today, it is the only way I
Can cling onto you

I have ripped off all my fingernails
Clinging on to you

Audrey, I don't get quite how
You swore to never forget me
Audrey, you said you'd never forget me
So, where the hell are you now?

SHE DIED ON THE STAGE

What an undeniable spectacle of tragic imagery
Holding her own arms for a lack of love
This is the immoral industry
She died on the stage, now she is up above.

The end of these days, it rests in needles and wine
Long black hair, not a second of a future in sight
I can't remember if she even finished one line
Vicious crowds stare and glare on a Serbian night.

She stood there, so lost. Like a comedian
Who was only ever met by laughter
When the ink dries for the tragedian
Life is so horrifying, so lonely forevermore after.

I should have stood beside her as she drifted away
She stumbled around the stage
I should have died beside her, that day
The day she died on the stage.

I am just like you
A silent action, so lost and afraid
To crave to be drunk or dead, either will do
To hear my own voice, in the way her broken tones swayed.

I know so well, the sound of the rain
The sound of cheers and screams
Of an audience, who will not listen to a single word of your pain
They should've done more for you, brought to life all your dreams.

Estranged jazz star of stage, far too much to discuss
I'm simply so sorry I couldn't help you
Separated jazz star of stage, who spelled out every word that for us
Are now so brutally apparent, so sickeningly true.

EVERY NIGHT IS NOVEMBER

Every night is November.
I am so very grateful for
The small piece of compassionate escapism
I was born to adore.
For no creature in reality,
No lukewarm flame, nor deep blue sea
Could shake the thorny days, modelled here

Nevertheless,

Every night is November.
The pat on the back of winter slowly crawling in
A taste of smoky surrealism
The flickering fire of the soul within
And Jean Valjean
Murmuring through his song
And the comfort in knowing, despite all that has gone wrong
Despite all that is going wrong,
She is out there
Maybe

Somewhere,

Every night is November.
Streetlights trickle in, with no rush or antagonism
Keyboard's roll, and catch the latch of the justifiably cold zephyr
The glee in the soul, of a November morning to follow
Wrapped and packed, in the blanket dark pink sky
Losing a grip of what is to beware
Almost distracted from the hell, that is really out there

Almost,

Every night is November.
And no matter the tug, or direction of the day
Each evening set to follow, the same electrifying formula
It's set to sit in this way.
And lean over my shoulder
Wrapping ill-meaning arms around me as I lay
The treacherously decorated mantlepiece of the mind, is ornamented
With violent flashes of faces, with all hell to pay
Not callous, nor disturbing, nor unnerving
The mark left on the brain

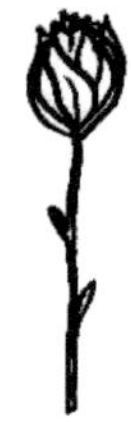

Although,

Uneasy contentment lay
In the heart of November
Such soul soothing cleansing warmth, shall never cease
The tangle of enraged light and frosty weather
Rain caves in, on rickety windows
The cheapness in the structure
Providing only a stalwart, sturdy thrill
As it lashes across the paintwork.
Perfect tones of how car tyres roll, rippling into place
Brings only such calming peace
They linger in comfort forever
As my heavy eyes are cradled by sleep
The ills of tomorrow, shall follow never

However,

POSTCARDS

Eerily, it is night
On the tight, twirly Victorian little road
Both months before and after the snow
Looming, gangly trees extenuate the shady grasp of the night
There is a meeting, in a secluded area
Between two secluded, separated hearts
As she enters the scene, reality departs.

He's not hiding away his face
He's so very happy to embrace
That old complexion of both hope and home
That quickly got away
How far is too far?
Your answer is written on a postcard.

Why in the year 8052 in the second December?
Are you still dreaming of her?
You got your day of fame
And then, of course, you lost it again
But it's somewhere hidden here, amongst the rubble
Written on a postcard, asking for trouble
Spilled out drunk, onto the table with
All of your past scars

She re-appears, and smiles
"Hello"
As if nothing at all had changed
And tells some nice stories
"You wouldn't believe what happened next"
To make it all, somehow, fit together
And make sense
To listen and believe is to ignore the present tense

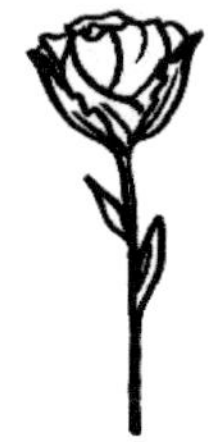

To ignore the past tense
"You mindless, unwise child!"
Tripped, fallen so far
Headfirst again.

A car windshield, shielding from the battering rain
Accelerate to Nottingham
Accelerate towards Notre Dame
Accelerate with me, anywhere, that isn't here.
Accelerate to Nottingham
Accelerate towards Notre Dame
Accelerate with me, anywhere. Take me anywhere.
Here in this dream
Wave eagerly the only true desires of this man
The long-lost, desires of this man

Hear her say
"Now he's gone, I love you"
Hear her silly voice say again
"Now he's gone, I love you
I love you
I love you
I love you."

So, you wrote your pompous little poetry
And sold your pompous little book
But it didn't solve anything did it?
You took all your thoughts
And you threw them to Jupiter, until you felt so alive
You wished you were dead
You published your tactless little book
And no one understood a single word you said
It didn't solve anything, did it?
The same state, with new haughty words
The answer is on a postcard

Hear her say
"Now he's gone, I love you"
Hear her silly voice say again
"Now he's gone, I love you
I love you
I love you
I love you."

So, you smiled and smirked
And felt mildly irked
That you had less days than nights
Time will always grasp and reappear
The very saddest days of your life
Have surely been and gone
The streetlights, leading on, tell you
There are still many more left to come

On the tight, twirly Victorian little road
Merge the terms bleed and bled
Fragile, emotionally bendable, to be teased and played
The trees change to postcards, until you suffocate
Your chest caves in
Again, heart open wide for the world to see
But this Victorian plain is conceived in the scheming eyes of she

The lights of the Victorian set crash your way and illuminate
Everyone claps and hollers, and laughs cruelly at you
You're just so desperate to ask
If any of the champagne-tasting madness was true
Eerily, it is day
As the curtains, the projection of the road is snatched away
But she is still there, for now.

Have you really been Mr Burbank all this time?
Open your eyes, remember you are wrong

Now, she is gone.
It's far too late to care about what's real
Does anyone really care what is real?
Your answer is on a postcard

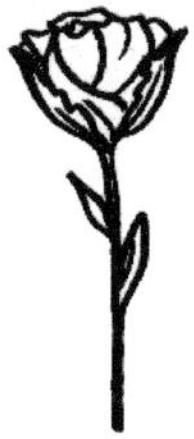

Your thoughts are all half-hoped delusions
But your tears, back on planet earth, are real
Your tears here and now, are real.

ALISTER ON THE ROOFTOP

I once said to my friend, "I am the answer"
Sprawled in three-year-old's writing
In black and white
And spoken in the doorways
Of eventual goodnights
And now, it's just...

Can you see
Alister on the rooftop?
Singing with sturdy power and grace, for the world to see
Alister singing, on the rooftop.

I'm ruling nothing out
I could still be alright
But admittedly, sometimes
I'm not 100% sure
If I'm even alive
And it's just...

Can you see
Alister on the rooftop?
Singing passionately, to you and to me
Alister singing, on the rooftop.

I hope it didn't last too long
All you have been through
I hope it didn't hurt as much
As these things, tend to do
Because, life is just...

Look closely enough, can you see
Alister dancing on the rooftop?

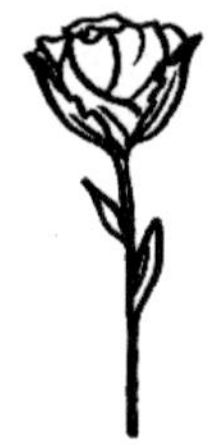

With Uranian majesty
Alister smiling on the rooftop.

And I'm smiling too
Isn't it strange?
How the world was set to be pleasant
And then it quickly changed
What is left, is just…

You can see
Alister on the rooftop
Swaying, happily lonely
Alister swaying on the rooftop.

And now you mention it
Yes, I remember you talking about
The space on the roof you'd sit and ponder
In the summer, on top of your house

Hello, again, my friend.
Do you remember the time?
Time was yours, and it was mine
And now it's just…

Look into my blue crying eyes
And can you see
Alister on the rooftop
Swaying, happily lonely
Alister swaying on the rooftop.

I once said to my enemy
Well, it doesn't matter, actually.
But when I see, Alister twirling on the rooftop
I know who I am and, who I will be
And now, it's just…

NEBULA

I fall to the floor with Irish violins and featherweight guitars
Menacing smiles stretch nearer, because of what is afar
You appear from the night sky; a knowing look in your eye
My heart sinks six feet deep and itches, to understand why.

Conjecture is briskly called to action
"Jump. Jump. Jump. And see what happens"
Your inability to let go, is so pure it borders on necromania
Encroached and approached by an overwhelming sense of wicked pyromania

Nebula, take me to the stars
Whatever we think is going to happen
Sadly, these things don't work out
The way we imagine

Nebula, do you know who we are?
Your attitude to love is *Fahrenheit 451*
I'm past the point of blessing
Alysha, you won't be young forever
And I am sure, you'll be taught this vital lesson

Nebula, lift me to the stars
Outgoing call - two minutes
The night stretches wide
And you don't know
I am dying inside

Nebula.
It's a shame you changed
Nebula.
Nebula.

I'm thankful for who you were to me
Sunrise, sunset, and all in between
You were rolling hills that welcomed May
It's a mighty shame you changed

And with those rolling summer hills in the afternoon
That embraced and kissed the warmth of June
I was me (probably) and
You were you
It's a shame that we changed

To listen and, be listened to
When the sun has set and
It's early AM, 3:52
In the morning
It's a bloody shame it all changed

From *'Funny Little Frog'*
To *'The Model'*
To *'Like Dylan in the Movies'*
It's a shame we
Are yesterday
It's a shame I went away

Nebula, near or far
Whilst I wake alone with a shiver and a scare
Go and chase all your dreams
I wish I could be there.

I sink to my knees
And Athena counts to three
You disappear on a temperate afternoon
And well. That was that.

Nebula, do you know who we are?
Your attitude to love is *Fahrenheit 451*
I'm past the point of blessing
Alysha, you won't be young forever
And I am sure, you'll be taught this vital lesson

From *'A Flash of Darkness'*, *'My Autumn Done Come'*
To *'Never Going Nowhere'*
To '*Roll Away*'
It's a shame we
Are days gone by
It's a shame I went missing

Nebula, near or far
Whilst I wake alone with a shiver and a scare
Go and chase all your dreams
I wish I could be there.

Nebula!
Nebula!
Nebula!
Near or far.

ON THE FLOOR OF THE EDITING ROOM

On the floor of the editing room
Is where you'll find my hopes and dreams
Drenched in the sunshine covering of disappointment
Is where you'll find all I have seen
And that unshakably stays with me

Left in days flying by
More of my mind is left deserted, imprisoned
Follow the drainpipes of houses on Yorkshire streets and
You'll find the chill of unease that has risen
To my chest

The shut-in air of that rotting, tainted pub
Is where you'll hear the gossip they've spread
If you travel long enough to be driven around the bend
You'll say the same words I have said
And know how I feel today

Enraging, engaging with reality
Is how hope is drained from minuscule, to none
In the downstairs cupboard, with the lights off
Is where I sit and miss what has gone
And miss what is still going on

On the sawdust coated wooden floor of the editing room
Is where I'll be
Today, tomorrow, and this time next week
Whenever you have the time
Please come and save me.

WHO'S HAPPY ENDING ARE YOU?

There's a nuclear bomb in your hometown
Ready to go off
And to splatter your grandfather back to when
Your love was good enough

Whether your thoughts are
Humorous, dark, slapstick or sharp
You'll end up drunkenly crawling
Through the streets, in the dark

Timothy wanted to smile and be free
And when whisky didn't work and the cat sold his bed
He took to the blinding lights of the stage and
Sliced off his own head

You might think an act of such public passion
Is a little drastic or crude
But
Who's happy ending, are you?

At half past two
The news began to filter through
And people scowled and howled
And called him a coward
You might agree with them
And stay here on planet Earth
Each day, scraping your gaze across Astroturf

You'll stay here on planet Earth
And you'll pretend that you are content

And that you are loved by MTV Unplugged
And that you're cherished, watching your enemies perish
And you're adored by a Oujia board
And you're favoured by semiquavers
And you're free in Los Angeles
And you're happy in Waterloo
But
Who's happy ending, are you?

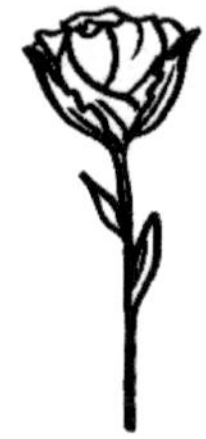

PROVEN RIGHT, AGAIN

Every step in this town
Is a slap across the face
A head-splitting fatal blow,
Onto the sullen street sign to this place.
Every step in this town
Is one giant slip backwards
To Victorian England.
Rain trickles; unnerving summer's day…

The heavy-light rain
Accentuates the colours of the day
And more and more, and more
The weather points the way
To hide behind the gale force
Of a metaphor.
My mind will lose a foreseeable fight
I'm terrified I'm
Going to be proven right.

Notice how it's a little darker,
A little earlier than before
Relief-less, unresponsive, riffed by night
As prowling around the bend, I cannot ignore
November looming with even sharper teeth
And sharper claws.
Each hour I feel, a little lonelier than before
I was Judas' condemned brother as
I strode home
Kicking my heart along the pavement…

I waited for the impact
And the burn at the side of the road

To hear the same old news
And throw away what progress had been grown.
Miss the night so very much
Remembering what it was like before
Feel the damage, the barrenness, the loss
For I cannot bear, to leave here tonight
To go somewhere, where you are not
To wander to nowhere, to feel each note
Of how scared I am, to be proven right.

This is a familiar feeling
But familiarity, brings no ease
Only worsening nights of tears
Battling whatever mind-crushing catastrophes, I please
I plead for them to stop
I find that darkness
Has many colours
If you stay here long enough
So, I beg and beg for connection
For anyone to help, and then I hear them talk…

They speak with a soft voice
(And that is nice to hear and know)
Yet it sharpens the itch for the blade
Life is a succession of voices you seldom want to hear
At the other end of the telephone.
And so, here waves
Incredible, implausible pain
Rip off the plaster, succumb to disaster
Just like the last, this storybook is burnt to flames
I am terrified to be proven right.

To be strung upwards, so damn high
Simply float away, careless, cuddled by the sky
Caressed carelessly, floating like a butterfly

But think of what plague will be left behind
There is no option other than
To drown in this whirlpool of goodbye
I stay awake
And think this way...

The fear of co-dependency
They're going to lock me up
Isolated lines
How much enough, before enough is enough?
I only have what I
Can barely hold in my hands
I feel the forceful, beseeching, begging screams of the child
With no ground left to stand…

Adding another five minutes
To the mind's nightly ritual
Another five minutes too many
The stare at 3am grows habitual
Under head-spinning, internal boundaries
Of both mortar, and brick
I lay, again and again
I lay and contemplate...

How time's tides sweep us off our feet
And I really have no advice for you
Other than to cling on, clench your jaw
And pray to your god you get through
Breathless in the beauty
Of the ease in which
Nature brings, and takes away life
Which, is why…

Blind faith in tomorrow
Saves my life

But, why?
Telling you that I love you
Saves my life
And I cry and I cry and cry
For what is to come
For I know I'll be proven right

The words have fallen out of me
And I have fallen on the floor
The sting left behind
I have written before
It is there
Dressed in black
And in white
I know I'll be proven right.

I'VE PACKED MY LAST COFFIN

I've packed my last coffin
I am still the screaming, insufferable light that summer handed to me
Stood with Billy Shears, who sneers around here
I know spaces of the mind you'd never wish to reach
Places you've surely seen in your dreams

"I can't stop thinking of all I've lost
She hated double maths on Tuesdays
The Daily Telegraph
And the strange skeleton men who read out the news
The future now goes on, with her
In the ground, embraced by the cold soil and
Laid with all the rest of them"

I've packed my last coffin
I am still the heart that cannot forget an unwritten symphony
The droning over the road, stood with Labi Siffre and his telephone
And that still really, truly upsets me very deeply
I cannot bare to hear his voice again

In this business, grieving feet are the ones that remain on the floor
Beaten Dominic, bullied himself sick
Guilt built into his lost African eyes; it was too late to ignore
As he said with a stuttering shake, "I love him more now
Than I ever could have before"

"I'm going to have to stop walking"
His legs became tired and bored of the repetitive stroll
With my anxious heart about to break
For the next observation I had to make
They beg and they beg and they beg, just for some happy news
As I am the one to contact the 'next of kin'

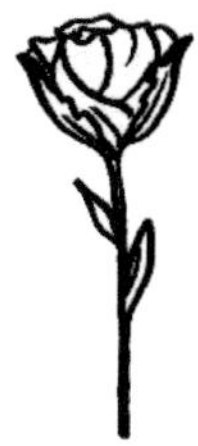

Whilst the Pet Shop Boys spit out *'It's a Sin'*
Such patchy, faded ink left in their name
Morality, no more solid than belief
How much longer will you be needing me?

My wholly dry eyes are starting to soften
Dressed, drowning and doused in Lynx Black
The facts are never really very fun
Is it better for the mind to be young, or the mind to be tired tattered and old?
The answer to this, even I do not know

Because for each happy day, there were ten sleepless nights
And the promises they made were very rarely ever kept
This is a path well-trodden, my fellow inmate
It is the dawn of yet another lonely day
There is nothing left to do, or to say
But drink myself into an early grave.

MAYBE I AM DEAD

Maybe I am dead
Maybe it's hellish flames that fuel this state of living
Here I am so cold and empty
As if the soul knows the life it is missing

Maybe I am dead
Maybe it all went to plan
And the fears felt by a spirit of the next world
Are just as absurd as those of a man

Maybe I am dead - all tears, all those years.
Marked in chalk on the streets
The peculiar gift of life now gone
The flair of days laid at your feet

Maybe I am dead
I hope so strongly this is true
There's a comfort you wouldn't understand
In losing everything I ever knew

I am still envious, open, and so terribly honest
For the girl in that deep and verdant forest
It has been far too many moons
Since I left this cocoon

Taste of despair, an infectious knell
Recalling first and last times
Inevitable final memories of mine
Maybe I am dead, and the plot of terror
Didn't dissolve, somehow
This I'm sure is the only way to explain who I was
And who I am now

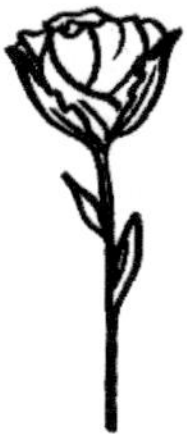

I don't want my youth anymore
Please tear it out of me
For in the survival's verse
I live in illiteracy
How do pages of the calendar still flip?
There has been too much time
Raindrops and tears still race one another
I have turned down your offer, of what is left to discover
They still sleep with fearless contentment
As the wonderstruck lay awake
They clutch at my ankles
Again, in such strain
Surely, I am dead?
It's the only explanation for this pain

Maybe I am dead
It has been far too long since I lost you
Please appear in any shape or form
Just tell me all this isn't true.

PENDULUM SWINGS

There's a murmur
Behind the wind-swept drift of the curtains
Pendulum swings.

Throw whisky on your cornflakes
And smiles on your mistakes
Pendulum swings.

Top of the Pops in 1980's December
No summer, all November
Pendulum swings.

What would she say
If she were here today?
Pendulum swings.

Nineteen types of smiles, only six mean joy
The clever soul's quest, is to crush and to destroy
Pendulum swings.

No matter how much optimism a heart can wield
It's difficult to walk to Wakefield
Pendulum swings.

Three kids, two bikes; the train-track is where Andy
Shall be strapped down tonight
Kill him! Kill him! For he cannot speak or sing!
Pendulum swings.

The voice and orchestra echo, in empty arenas
As light draws out, delusion increases
Pendulum swings.

Hiding deep in the shade
From the mistakes I have made
Pendulum swings.

Soul soars
Heart pours
Pendulum swings.

Time makes anything
Impossible to hold
Time makes anyone
Just impossible to hold
Pendulum swings.

“When she smiles”
I die
Pendulum swings.

Kill him! Kill him!
For he cannot speak or sing.
Pendulum swings.

LITTLE BAG

I have a little bag where I keep,
The next mountain to climb, one a little too steep
Melancholy last days of summer, freefalling
Into the open arms of autumn.

I have a little bag where I keep,
My terror at anything cruel
Happy people
And the television news.

I have a little bag where I keep,
Nights where my mind ceases to sleep
Pockets of resentment walk in blood-soaked sheepskin
You have no idea of the pain I am in.

I have a little bag where I keep
Music played loudly
Complete confusion
And unknown identity, displayed proudly.

Trying to make sense of this mess
A wandering child with
The incurable curse
Of loneliness.

I have a little bag where I keep,
A spiral of white lies, drowning too deep
The familiarity of a fallen tree
And all the times when I knew you didn't love me.

I have a little bag where I keep,
A time where I was a mythical mystery, too clumsy to creep

A boy taken for granted, left with too much time to think
Now I am here, and all I did was twice blink.

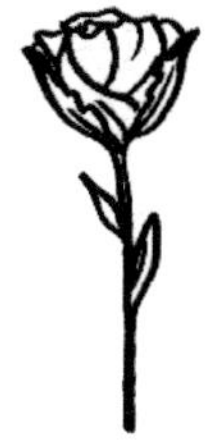

I have a little bag where I keep,
Good luck smiles, advice from teachers in school
Of how I must take joy from the little things
(And now, good lord, are they minuscule)

I have a little bag where I keep,
The voice in our heads, that begs us to leap
And that I have to, I have to, I simply must let you know
Exactly what you already know…

My mind was made to bend and to break,
With a stun, a shiver, and a poisoned liver
Never, blissfully drift away
Stay awake, stay awake, stay awake
Stay awake
Stay…

THE WORLD WOULDN'T WANT TO LOSE ME

When it's dark, the bleak streets get lighter
That has never once happened to me
Smell the dried blood, eyes alive and brighter
A reminder, of where you've been.
The sweep of the streets isn't any funnier
In sunshine, I am not warmed
The tide of time no longer appears linear
In nostalgic cries, I am warned.

Memoirs can be written, with a cheap or expensive pen
That isn't the case for me
Though, you might pass by now and then
A reminder of who you've been.
Into my skinny arms fell the time
Often, a crowd welcomed my words with arms wide
I gleefully choked upon every line
But I wasn't laughing inside.

I never thought
When I said
"Take my secrets to the grave"
You'd take that quite so literally.

Each day was a wild, uncouth frenzied
Hatred filled performance
Both unconventional and unenvied
For my own quiet reassurance
But now, Marvin galloping in spring
The despairing laugh of sadness fuelled hate
And so many other things

Must wait. Be left to disappear, to dissipate.

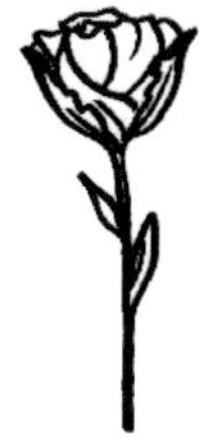

Each day, see this face again, and instinctively yawn
I always make the same moves across the board
And, lovely, after all those sentiments half withdrawn
You're bound to have grown bored
I know it was my fault.
Past strengths, are always the strongest
Unhappily, I am pushed aside
What happened first, has gone on the longest
Alas, the ease of new goodbyes.

Just sometimes
When I remember
Looking, in your eyes
I thought you would miss me.

A sense of freedom beckons, waiting
In shades of green and grey, over the horizon
But in these times cage bars, shaking
Only grip and further tighten.
My nightmares happen when I wake, no way to be free
I hit the trunk, not the leaves of the tree
Though, the world wouldn't want to lose me
No matter how many times, I have tried to flee.

Dusk, troubling crying sky
So easy on lonely eyes
Unsteady, unstable, spilling rumour
Gather 'round the fire, in the name of gallows humour.
So, laugh instead
Please, go ahead
And let the pain dwell, for right or for wrong
Let it sit in the heart, for all too long

With the worst concluded
Now begins the rest of my life
Though, we know, it is foolish to think
Any story is over.

The world wants to keep me, for the next seven summers
I have so often, very nearly made the right decision
But, how many others
Can mourn the still living?
Who can walk around, without a slant of anguish showing?
A person to be lost, but never missed
With the intelligence, the awareness of knowing
Happiness simply doesn't exist.

The children shriek as they are born
They know what is coming next
Stich after stich after stich
On the jumper of goodbyes.

Line lost, coated in frost
Too often this has happened to me
Only further flashes in the mind of suicide, left to attain
But the world wouldn't want to lose me
So, I must fall flat on my face, again.
The key to eternal life
Is simply wanting to die.

WHEN THE SKY IS LIGHT AND BLUE

When the sky is light and blue
The grass, vibrantly green
The outside a fresh, calm routine
Satisfaction: the day teases me

Nowhere particularly to go
And nothing particularly to do
No desire to know what is so, and what is untrue
A tranquil space alone, a room with a view

Walls never to be re-visited
Paths and avenues no longer mine
Laid alone in solace, drenched in sunshine
With a gentle grip on time

No sign of you, here with me
Or on the other end of the telephone
Alone on my deathbed, I am ready to go home.

NOTHING IS EVER FORGOTTEN

I heard a song you wrote
It has touched and torched my world ever since
I heard your voice, on the telephone
My lungs ceased to breathe

I heard your sweet voice on the telephone
A birdsong, cast away for years
When you left me down the aisle in June
I would've given my whole life to you

I heard your voice again
A reminder, of how you will never again arrive
And now, God knows
As summer came
And fell away again
I am boy estranged

But I haven't changed
I haven't changed
I promise, I am the same
I'm still the same
I heard your voice again
It was your voice and
I heard it again

As winter came
And scowled again
I haven't changed
Nothing is ever forgotten
I'm still the same.
Come back
And love me again.

The brother of death
When and where I was enough
When and where those who are gone, return, to be with you
When and where the smooth isn't outcried by the rough
When and where you don't have to lie
Where all emotions are real
Where you are allowed to cry
Elusive to the weight of time
Bliss in darkness
The answered call of life
When for now, I will suffice
Nothing is ever forgotten; escape
Nothing is ever forgotten
Nothing is ever forgotten
Nothing, nothing, nothing.
I am ready to be taken

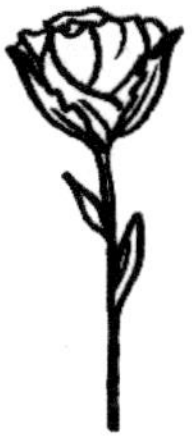

Take me.

As summer came
And fell away again
I am boy estranged

But I haven't changed
I haven't changed
I promise, I am the same
Nothing is ever forgotten
I'm still the same.
Come back
And love me again.

SUCCINCT SUCCESS

His brown eyes opened, and he smiled
He believed life
Could not feel any worse
The train had departed
It was around then
The nausea started

The worst days of his life
Made him feel no better at all
His brown eyes opened
And he dreamed he stood tall
His eyes opened wide

And the happiest days of his life
Weren't even particularly happy
His brown eyes opened
And he smiled
And he laughed
He really laughed
One day soon
It shall not be June
His brown eyes opened

His brown shoes opened
They did not smile
They are shoes.
The shoes walked away
Try to walk away from this mess
Without your shoes
Try to walk without limbs
Walk without my limbs
Let there be no more tears

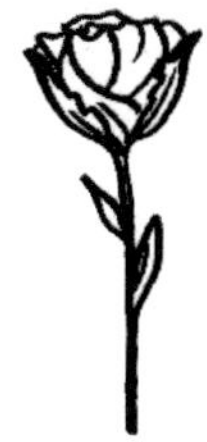

For there have been too many
Already
No more tears
No more fears
Too many
To walk without your limbs
Talk without your chins

"I want to take everything I have away
I want to stop
To rot
Away"
Nevertheless
His brown eyes opened
And he pretended to smile
Sending his loving family on their way
Back many miles
Remembering
His brown eyes
Which, undoubtably
As you know
Opened, and he smiled

He never gets to say goodbye
He never gets to say goodbye
I never got to say goodbye
I never got to say
Hello.
I never got to say
His brown eyes opened and he smiled

He was a withered, wrinkled and loathsome visage
A loathsome visage
Loathsome visage
Wholesome facade

His brown eyes smiled and he opened
His brown eyes
His brown eyes opened, and he smiled
His brown eyes opened, and he smiled

MAY I RECOMMEND SILENCE?

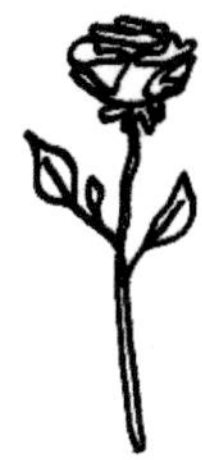

Labels do all but free and liberate
Labels live to ground and fascinate
The cavern of the dark ominous soul of deep
Deep unhappiness

Boxes to tick and for you to be placed
Boxes to send your bipolar sister into outer space
Come along, give all your hate, why must you have
So much hate?

Gatherings to sit around, and to garishly smile
Gatherings to wish you were a few thousand miles
In any other
Direction at all

Find an identity to fit in, just to be punished
Find an identity so unique, you fly the same kite
As everyone else
In the room

Walk away from me, to pursue happiness
Walk away from me, a quest for manly womanliness
I am my punisher, handsome crucifier
I am
Pretending I'm undecided
As that hurts far less
Than the decision I have made.

HILLARY'S SOLILOQUY

"I have not said 'good morning'
Or 'goodnight'
In such a long time
Each day, I'm sure the clouds go by
But I rarely ever notice
The past is a silk carpet
Stretched out, hazy and wild

I live in the midst
Of the sole breeding ground
For all desperation in the universe
Grime sprawls on the walls
With dejection
Lustfully longing to be bombed into extinction
At every passing moment
The decaying stench of each day
Creates and constantly generates
Sinister nightmares
It is easier to give in
Lay on the rooftop and whisper to the sky
'Please enter; join me in my dreams
If you haven't already'

The morning that rises
Just 24 hours after the last
Is always the same
It's here to offer an unwanted gift
An unwanted gift of wretched delay
Of being taken away
By the hearse
For some, that day will spell

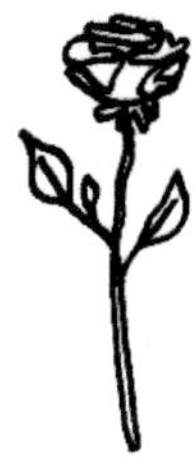

A tremendous waterfall of crocodile tears
Lined with sequins and ceremonial fondue
For others, no one at all shall notice
This does not matter
Due to the unbreakable mould of this venture
Death is such a liberating fate

This town is a legless child
In the shallow end
Pretending not to drown.
This town is the poster boy
For anti-depressants.
This town is the girl
With legs far too heavy
To be supported by the floor.
The ceiling is waiting
To crash down
And to kill us all
A place where one's best hope
Is to walk fast and shamelessly
Right out of the front door
But forget to open it first

Murders of crows visit here only once
Before swiftly departing
Searching for any other place
Less stiflingly gothic
Their wings in flight
Are the closest physical representation
Of the freedom and the spirit
Those people who pass underneath them
Shall never have
They glance in my direction, from time to time
Fluttering over the rooftops
Passing over the other houses around here

Where the children hang and play
On broken chandeliers

The pedestrian people that pass by
Are all celebrating some special anniversary
Of the time, they were captured
By one illusion or another
Was it love?
Was it death?
Narrowly avoiding death?
It's just another day, really
The past is all we are
It's just another day
Another day I have the profound pleasure
Of sitting and slowly watching time waste away
Strength of such emotions evoked
Through this delightful marvel
Are rather impolite
Nonetheless, there is no alternative
Other than to battle with the mundane
And make no mistake
Nobody ever wins, against time

They spend £1000 at Murder King
And then twice as much at the gym
I no longer understand anything.
And the few jewels, who light up the room
Have less than a second to speak
What happened to listening?
Responding without advice or pleasantries
Just. Listening.
And taking comfort in knowing
There is at least one person in the world
Who is also in the quicksand
But holding your hand

Whilst watching the geese glide above
Where has this gone?
They were with you in the quicksand
But then, of course
Gone
To be one with the silent mob
As if you'd never even met
Once holding your hand in the quicksand
Now a stranger, a black clock on a
Murky November night.

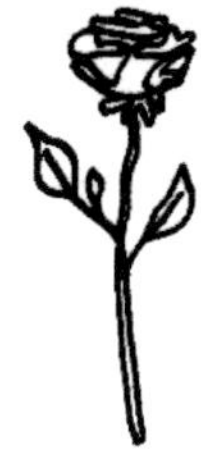

There is always one stoned girl
With her head in the kitchen sink
I watch cautiously from afar
And she makes my stomach sink
There is always one stoned girl
Her words at this time of the night
Are both clumsy and thin
Yet, somehow
They mean everything
They're everything she's ever wanted to say
They're all I have ever wished to say
Hidden behind socially maladroit staggering and turbulent fray
Lay words and sentiments
Ones of real pain
She, like me, is pain

Progression is an obsession
By those who are going nowhere
To live by numbers, a calendar
Soon, Monday the 12th
Turns into, 'I wish you good health
But, please kill yourself'
Tomorrow is just another unkept promise
For the rare few who are somehow

Really, truly connected
They never seem to say hello
The best they can hope for
Is to get to say goodbye
Those big white discoloured doors revolve
But nobody ever leaves

These feelings are *'Que Sera Sera'*
In the ears of the head spilt sideways
After it's skull smacks across the tyres
These feelings are if children's films
Had authentic endings
A break from the sand and sea
The sunshine and the smiles
These feelings are an ironed shirt
Perfectly placed
For the day that didn't take place
These feelings are
A steady slumbering stutter to the gallows
For the child-like eyes
The killer in the Harrington jacket

The past is a white straitjacket
Splendidly unfashionable
Curiously repressed, tightly strung
A place to never go back
But still
As always
A temptation."

SIBYL VANE IS DEAD!

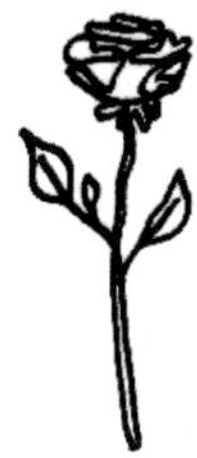

Just too many wrongs, not so many rights
Just too many peculiar, screaming nights
But at last, at last, at last
Sibyl Vane is dead.

Just too many very pretty, lonely goodbyes
Just too many half-baked, humble pies
But at last, at last, at last
Sibyl Vane is dead.

Again, words lay in twisting knives
One too many, gripping skies
Just too long writing a review
Far too long knowing you
But at last, at last, at last
Sibyl Vane is dead!

Just too much sunshine and sea
Far too many passing eyes and repressed glee
Trapped under venerable debris
Why, speaking now in the royal we?
But at last, at last, at last
Sibyl Vane is dead!

Just too many lines, that made too much sense
Just too many times, evaluating the present tense
Far too many near misses, between needle and thread
Thank God, she is dead.

Sibyl Vane is dead!
Sibyl Vane is dead!
At last, at last, at last
Sibyl Vane is dead!

GUILT

I was 16 when the sun forgot to rise
Streetlights on full-beam
In the daytime
I came home to find
His dead remains
Cast across my bed
Like sybarite lungs
Ragged to threads
I can't ever again
Face myself.

The guilt wades through the morning
In flutters
Flowing smoothly, softly
A knife through butter
To view its hues of blue fade away
Fade to crisp and cold brown
Exhibits the pain I know
Of the world around.

To then, sit alone
And watch the streets
Calm and tranquil
Love is locked between the concrete
Summer moonlight and night time
They wander with the stars
They bring back reminders
Of all the scars
All the speeding cars
And how
I got to be here now.
Soon, police sirens
Shall replace
Violins.

FLEET STREET

When you've achieved all of your goals
And all of your dreams
Where in hell will he be?

Once you've tasted cheap, watered-down vodka
And the safety space of that bubble, of that place
You won't even remember
His name, or his face

When your ambitions are realised
And all of your tears have dried
How many times will he, have failed and tried?

Once you've lived in most pleasurable chaos
And showered smiling, in the rain
What use to you
Is his face, or his name?

What use to you
Is his face, or his name?

A SONNET FOR WEDNESDAY AFTERNOON

As you lay awake all night, with your fingers crossed,
Waiting for any excuse to abort the mind's sickening solitude relay
Please remember, nothing good is lost,
It's just a little further away.

When the day comes where this loneliness is buried in sand,
And they all want your autograph
Keep your hands by your side and
Try not to laugh.

There is only sunshine in your path
No matter which way the river sways
Embrace the waves of contentment in the aftermath
Or feel however you must, living beneath changing rays.

Just don't align your pain with mine,
By feeling left behind.

OCTOBER 24TH

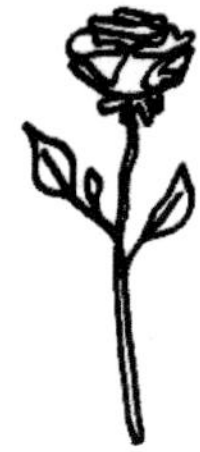

Inspired by Anne Sexton's 'December 1st'

Holding a brain that's heavier
Than an empty page,
I think I'm softening
In my young age.
With all I have to give and say
Left behind, somewhere backstage
Far too tired, too empty
To be filled with regret and rage,
I think I'm softening
In my young age.

Daily punches in the stomach
Are affecting my productivity
Art gives me freedom
In absolute captivity.
A secret no one cares to know
How I sleep in brittle sensitivity
Voiceless optimist
I smile with absolute selectivity,
This is freedom
In absolute captivity.

I DO MY ADVENTURES ALONE

On these paths,
I am docile and passive
There is no need for them to understand
Or for my hands to grasp it
To watch the passing, glancing eyes
What the hell is within?
I do not need to know
For I do my adventures alone.

Around these terraced houses
The sequins on the ceiling
Converge to roll and fold
And even the dust,
Is two million years old
The people underneath, pretend to be
What they'll never, ever be
This has never been me
The only outlines drawn are my own,
For I do my adventures alone.

The spirits of the unspeakably lonely
In solitude grasp and hold me
I could only ever
Go on these journeys alone
We can play the game
If you like
And I'll pretend
It'll all work out fine
It shall not, it cannot, it is not. . .

To pass and smile at the locals
Covered in the natural pride of prescription bifocals

The look on their face, is always the same
They glance, as if to say
"Isn't it a shame we are here."

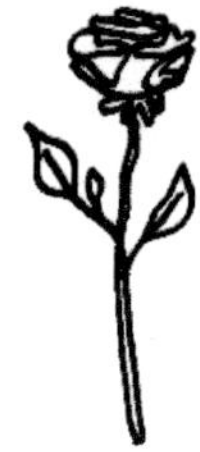

Therapeutic, liberating
Yet wholly heart-breaking
I smother my skin on the glass
On a quest to solve the questions
Nobody had ever even asked
And the blue car that follows me around
It knows the traits of the child
"It is such a shame, the meaning of your smile"

I do my adventures alone
I visit the graves
Of where nobody even died!
The voices, carved in wood say
"Isn't it such a shame
You are still here"

The expiry date on life
And on living
Are not always the same
I have no acts left to perform on this stage
Though, my moment to die
Has been and gone
In weakness,
And in strength
Survival is the only option I have left.

HAVE YOU YET MET JENNY?

There is something so very strange
About people who are happy
Tell me now with certainty
Have you yet met Jenny?

She is such wonderful company, with her expensive lipstick
And sad heavy eyes, that hang like a beagle's
She'll explain to you how
Happiness is for normal people

Normal people
With dreams and ambitions
Haircuts and wishes
And wonky satellite dishes

Have you yet met Jenny?
And told her all about who I am
Teased by my own existence and
The world's least wanted man

There is no finer therapy than bad singing
I am sure she is the very best there is
Go! Go! Spread your wings and be free
Watch sadness ripple, as bubbles fizz

Have you yet met Jenny?
As you said so often you would
And told her about who I am
The boy with the crooked back, living in the mud

Last night was the worst of my life
As all my worries and pains were realised

By thrilling colours of moving motorway dreams, where
The compressed pain of a heart is illuminated, and
emphasised

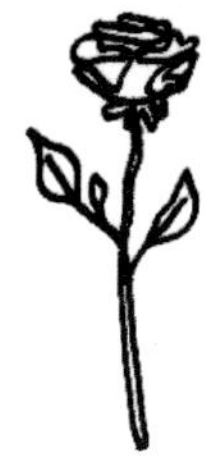

I can't afford to go to the opticians
In case they make me see things clearly
Tell me the future we planned is true, give me some hope
Have you yet met Jenny?

Last night was the worst of my life
As all my worries and pains were realised
In the shape of the legless trauma
That floated above me, in the sky

I heard that, just last week
You had quite the encounter with Jenny
It has come with pain, yet little surprise
To know you never mentioned me

I heard that, just last week
You confessed your love to Jenny
There is something so very strange
About people who are happy.

WILL YOU?

Will you leave me fixated, wrapping words around my mind?
Leaving trinkets of pure joy for me to find
Will you print a smile on my face each sunrise, knowing you are near?
And make gentle, devoted words so crisp and so clear
Will you make me feel as though I am heard and seen?
Create a true *'Midsummer Night's Dream'*
Will you see me smile as summer clouds fly by?
As one hundred and one joyful years go by
With you.
Will you want me, and soon cast me aside?
As quickly as anyone lived and died
Will you leave me gasping for air?
As the addict I am, smoked with despair
Will you leave my neck hung from a branch?
Via means of a solitary disappointed glance
Will you leave me here as I am, alone?
Belittling all once said and once shown
Will you?

Will you drag me to the canal, in your soft arms?
Painting a glorious evening of unity and calm
To my greatest fears, will you respond, "never"?
Or will you think of others when we are together
Will you run free and happy, around, and around?
Or will I be the boy at home, dragging you down
Will you fill me with security, or leave me a frightened mess?
Pointless, soulless, lifeless and above all, useless.
Will you?
Will you please track me down and call my bluff?
I am pointless, soulless, lifeless and above all, not enough.
I am where you will leave me, find me if you care or can

Alone is where I am
Is love the solution, or the problem?
Alone is how I am
With you.

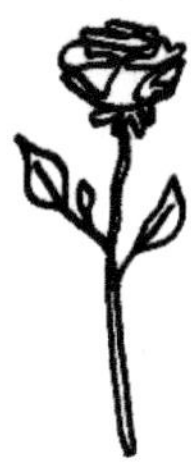

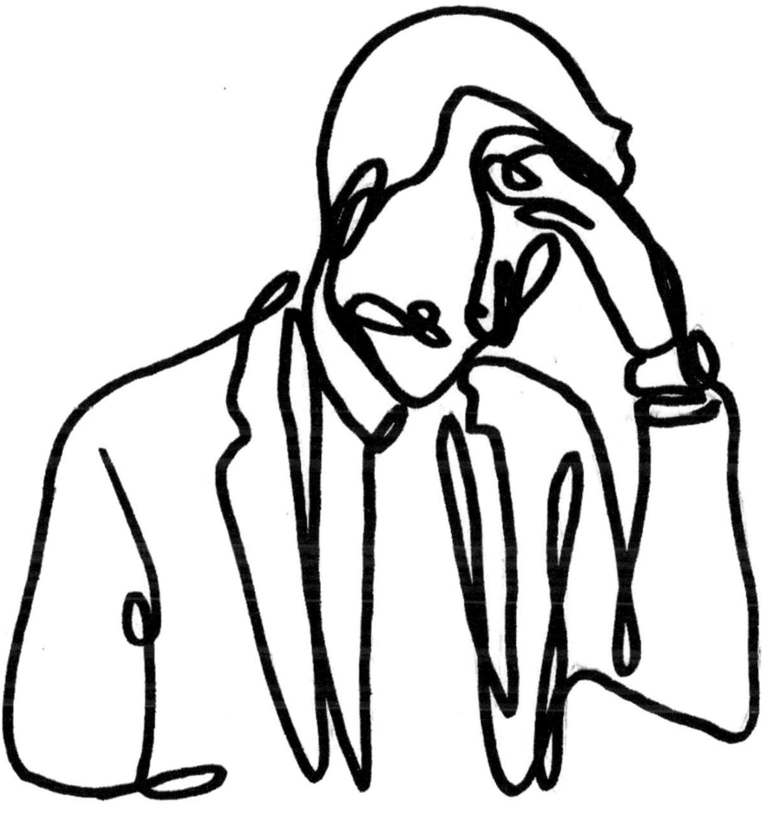

END OF SECTION A

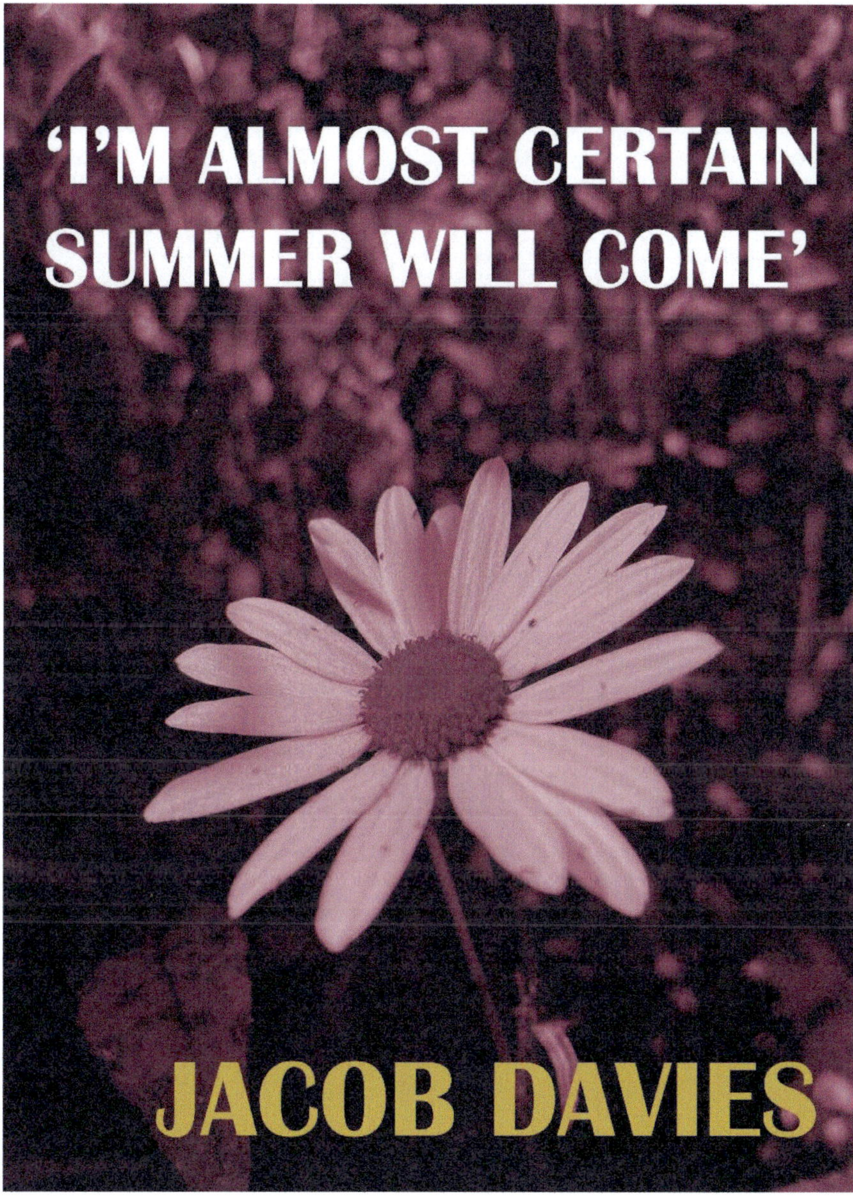
'I'M ALMOST CERTAIN
SUMMER WILL COME'
JACOB DAVIES

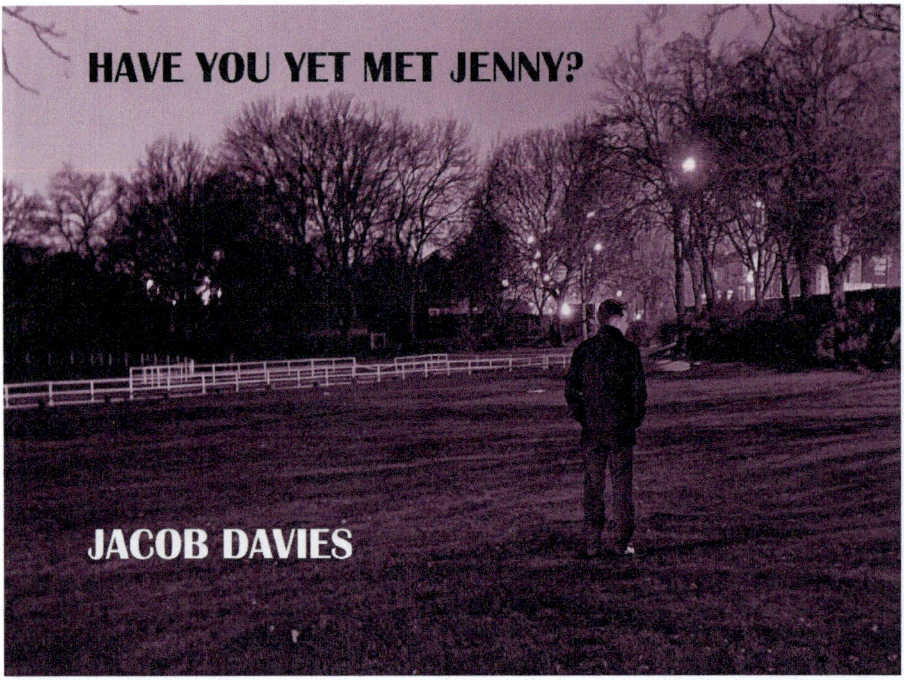
HAVE YOU YET MET JENNY?
JACOB DAVIES

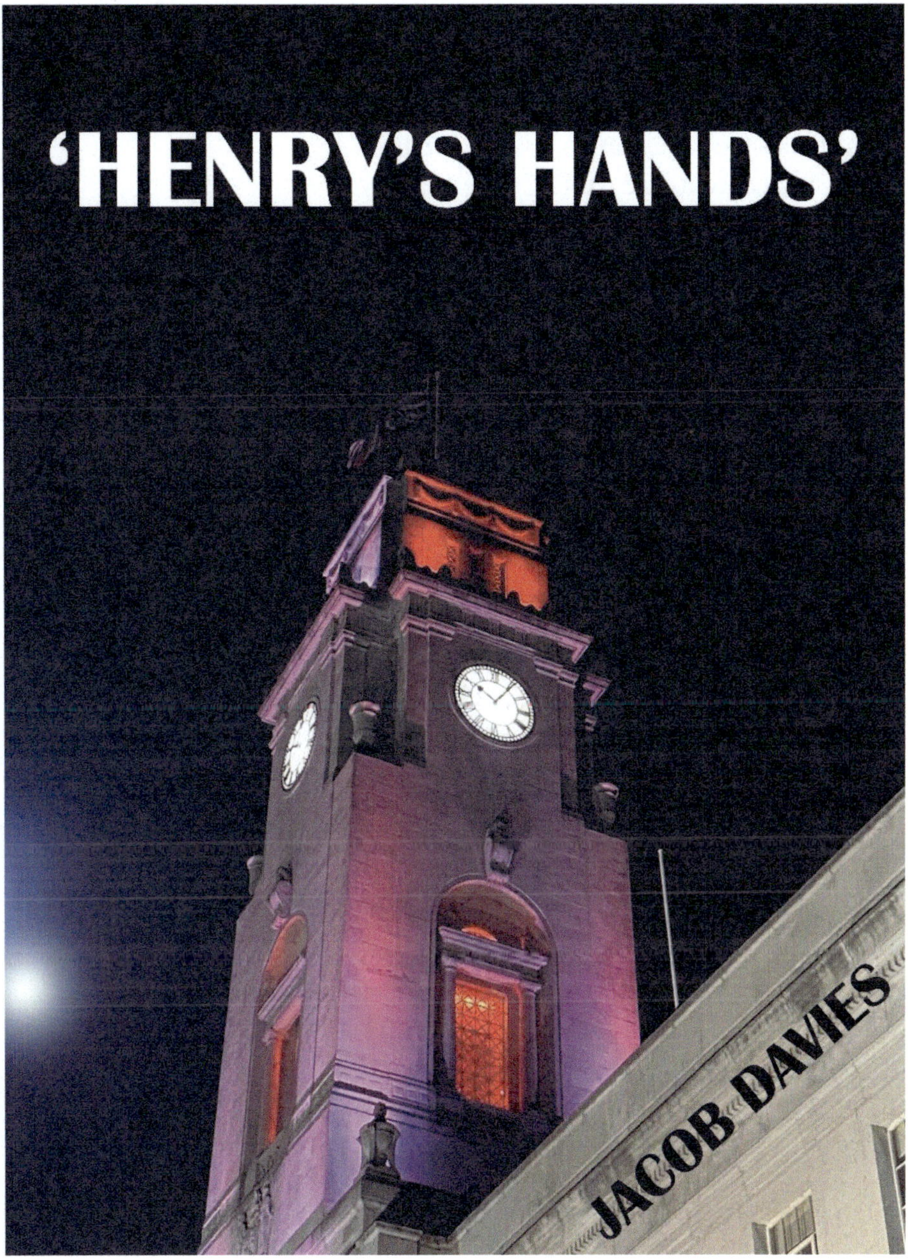
'HENRY'S HANDS'
JACOB DAVIES

SUNDAY, SHORTLY AFTER

RIP Clifford and Joy
Engulfed by the acceleration of dread and
Days of macabre desire; smiles that were coy.

RIP April; who drank a litre of wine
And who suffered the consequences of sleep schedules
That did not align.

RIP Winter; as longingly lonely as a blood-thirsty dove
Who lived to embrace ignorance, nastiness, manipulation
Or a combination of the above.

RIP Chris; Who passed simply to annoy
His mind, always an open void and shrine to indecision
Of how time spelt corrosion of joy.

RIP November's shadowy face; now up above
How scandalous that one should not be happy
Whilst "in love"

RIP Vivian; who walked incongruously briskly
She walked home
Into sabotage-flavoured whisky.

RIP Daisy Hadtogo; so patiently she waited
She cried and begged to go
Where Chris had been cremated.

RIP black and red soul
As Hypnos and Thanatos held hands
Gentle piano tunes, still roll.

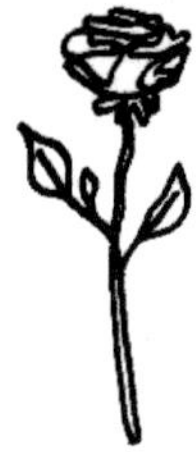

RIP fast car, sharp bend; shut eyes, engaged clutch
For someone who knows everything
I don't know very much.

RIP Coalition Carlisle; So bowled over
So awestruck
By her creased Jeremy Corbyn poster.

RIP Mary; she walked for hours in the rain
'The whiskey didn't kill the pain'
She walked for hours through the streets and lanes.

RIP Easter; dropped dead; she did nothing wrong
Life has a tendency
To go on and on and on.

RIP Grace Less; who only ever made friends
In very dark places and
At arm's length.

RIP Naomi
Now she is gone I wouldn't even bother
Getting to know me.

RIP Death; long live his successors name
April still calls the ways
History still today, paints his fame.

RIP John Palmer; "my last gloomy friend"
I knew then as my knees began to tremble
On York cobbled streets, that was his end.

RIP Ivory Roses
To the sit with the shore in her eyes
The colour of the ocean was chosen

RIP Dolores away she flew
Here in twenty, twenty, twenty
Twenty, twenty-two

Dolores Died!
Surely you can see the tears
In my eyes

Dolores died! Dolores died!
After, I laid down and cried
For at least forty minutes
Or possibly, forty-five

Dolores died! Dolores died!
Gone from restless to restful, good and proper
She was always there for me, likewise I
Was for her, though I had very little to offer

Dolores died! Dolores died! Dolores died!
I can die happily now that
There's a line in my book I'm making
With your memory etched upon it
One that I'm sure, will be mistook and mistaken

Dolores died! Dolores died! Dolores died!
Nothing! I am you.
Nothing, I cannot bring you warmth or security
Or bring you love and freedom
Or bring you back to me

Dolores died!
I never told her I heard that song and found that photo
I glanced with a sigh… it feels like yesterday
And at the same time… it feels like tomorrow

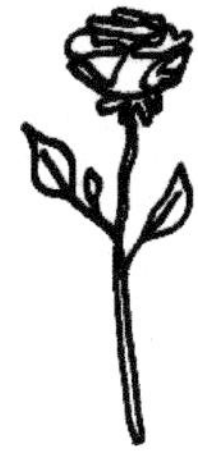

Dolores died! Dolores died!
But still, I would throw myself backwards
Into blind and obsessive affection
If you so much as glanced, once again
In my direction

Dolores died! Dolores died! Dolores died!
Pigs could take off and fly
And Father Christmas could clutch his frosty chest and die
Before I could face that…

Dolores died! Dolores died! Dolores died! Dolores died!
Your hair could spin away and fly
And I could die, at least once or twice
Before I could understand why…

Dolores died! Dolores died!
Just like me
You too, my friend
Have a place on the guillotine

Dolores died!
Surely you can see the tears
In all of our eyes…

"A sense of comfort only you can bring, and despite
The little it is worth, on my part
You have restored the dying art
Of love at first sight

For your happiness, I shall willingly haul on the front line
For your life is worth far more than mine
Tell me we'll both just be sat here
In one million years

I have died! Under each and every star
One thousand times
It has only got my trembling hands this far
I have died and loved and died
Tell me we'll both be smiling here
In fifty billion years
I have died
Won't you come join me?
Won't you join me?"

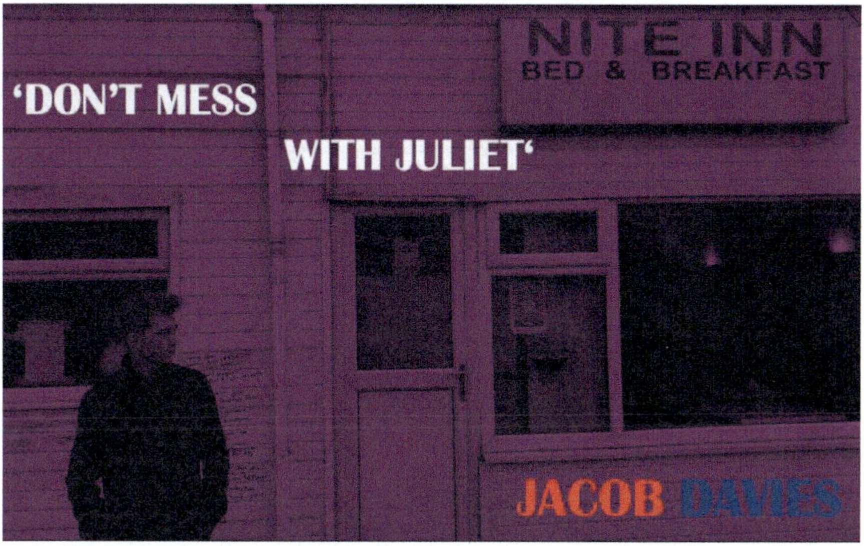
NITE INN
BED & BREAKFAST
'DON'T MESS
WITH JULIET'
JACOB DAVIES

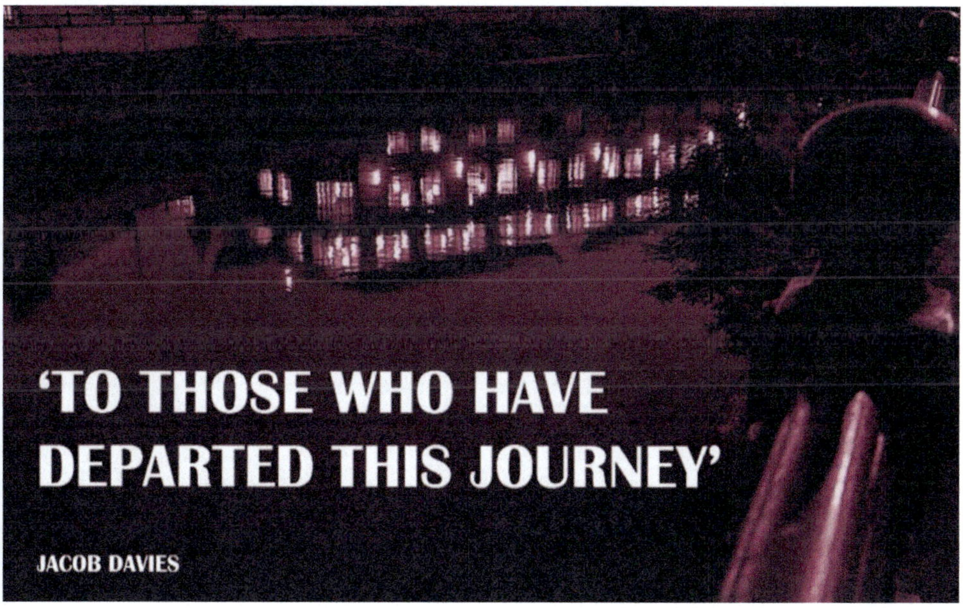
'TO THOSE WHO HAVE
DEPARTED THIS JOURNEY'
JACOB DAVIES

Alone.
The chords roll on.
The years go on
And this is why
I am not them

SECTION B

THE BUS HOME TOGETHER

Ideas that appear, and are clear, in the mind
Have become the most disturbingly rare things to find.

Don't you worry your poor, frightened soul about me
You can get the bus home together, to sand or to sea
And I'll stay standing and smiling here, on my own forever
Ghostly loneliness, when classical music goes on, for a little too long

I have tasted joy; instantly flatlined and died
An open void, false pretence, almost as if
happiness
was
busy
Until the whole world felt unsteady and dizzy
Ideas that appear, and are clear, in the mind
Have become the most disturbingly rare
Things
To
Find.

Ideas that appear, and are clear, in the mind
Have become the most disturbingly rare things to find.

By all means, walk away, walk away, walk away
You can get the bus home together, to useless bay
I shall stay alone, reciting lines of Macbeth; freezing to death
You have no use for my advice, reassurance or crashing flashbacks, even though I

Have tasted loneliness; languishing on my tongue
On days went on for months and months and months
Punch

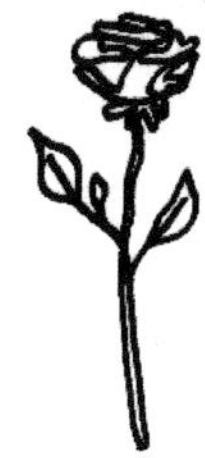

after
punch
So many promises, each day of a free lunch
Ideas that appear, and are clear, in the mind
Have become the most disturbingly rare
Things
To
Find.

Ideas that appear, and are clear, in the mind
Have become the most disturbingly rare things to find.

Why now am I
So easily swept aside?
It's a truth you'll ignore, but one you cannot hide
Foreseeable deterioration, bites with no remorse
Nature's insatiable taste for heartbreak, takes course
Leaving only incongruous conversation
Burning, within
And fiery hell, without sin

The empty room
Is filled with an air of solitude-brushed disappointment
For the night that could've been
Your empty smile, now distant by many miles
Fills me with frustration
For this outcome, I should've seen
Because you know, that I

Have tasted unity; bitter and quickly turned sour
I'd love to indulge in how I felt again, in the
First
Quarter
Of an hour
It all seemed so peaceful, then down came the towers

Ideas that appear, and are clear, in the mind
Have become the most disturbingly rare
Things
To
Find

Ideas that appear, and are clear, in the mind
Have become the most disturbingly rare things to find.

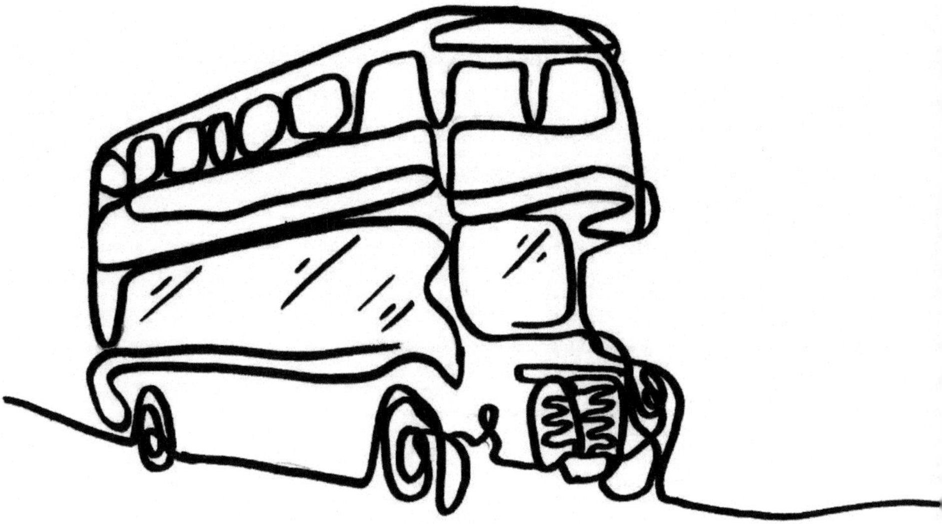

WRITTEN ON A PAVEMENT

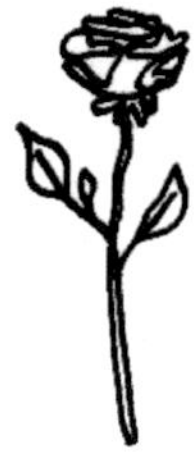

How many pills will do the job?
To put in action the end
Of the shame and the pain
Of who I should be

How many spills are left until I slip?
Into the coma to solve all worry
Worry to twist, turn and shun away
The person I could've been

How many films have to clip, reel into flames?
Before the warmth reaches anywhere near my heart
Hurt carefully placed between the pages
Of the book I couldn't finish

How many words are left before you?
Live the tomorrow that comes after we part
Expectations and realisations, guilt, all can be fixed
But not the human heart.

WHEN I SAW YOU IN A PRADA JUMPER

When I first saw your face,
I knew they must've run out of space
At the cemetery
When I saw you cry at the alter
With enough tears to bathe all of Malta,
I saw the rest of my life…

When I first saw your skewed grin,
I knew each syllable of the state
I'd always be in
When I saw you in a Prada jumper, begging for a fiver
And careering around like a drunken driver
I saw the rest of my life…

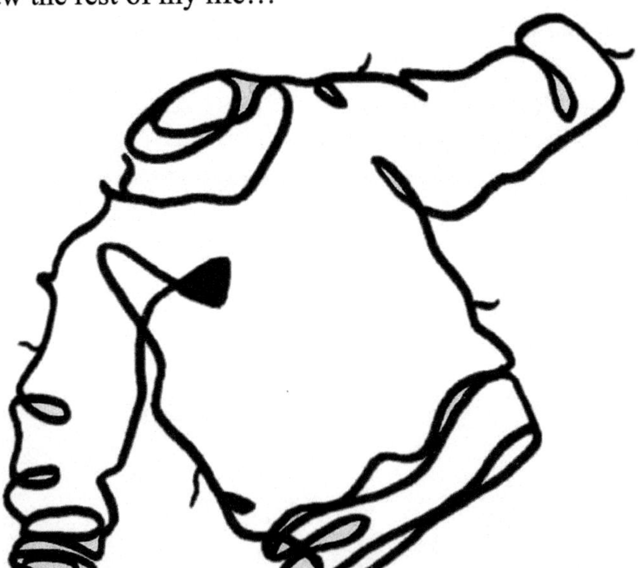

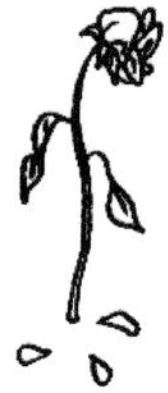

Here is burning today!
Pouring hell, no ceasefire
Here. Lay. Final. Desires.
I am nature's doorstep
And nature's floor
Silently.
I am the grass I adore
Tremoring terrain
Here is who I am
Here is forevermore

Here is smoke rising!
I cannot breathe
Past bleeding to future
Each evicted and
Fantasised twig
Spread my tired wings
Sprawl on the ground
I shall be where
It cannot ever
Find me now

Here is
Sleep's gentle pressing!
High enough to be above
Low and small
Enough to fall
Darkness is
Exponentially
Expensively crushing
Contentment, is unknown
Woes, ways
Of decrepit hands, on show

Here are
Violent screeching cuts!
No longer
Aligning straightly
"I have been sleeping
Badly lately"
The smell of blood
Vomits over the bathroom
Thoughts inside the head,
Boy in the afternoon

Here is me!
I am one with
The foliage!
I need no more than
To lay on the grass
And forget, forget
When my silly face
Hadn't yet fallen into place
Invited to
A search party
For my missing
Sense of reality
Freshly saved and
Freshly shaved
And freshly whacked
Around the face
Drinking acid and
Seeing Jesus himself
Pick up a copy
Of 'The Pleasures of the Damned'
From the crooked
Dust-bitten shelf

Here is me!
Yes!
Here I am!
Here is the moon!
I wake up early
Arrival of the gloom
The rest of my life
Such empty
And dry afternoons
Sickening fear
To forever live that June
Here is June!
Incantation of the wind won't relent
For neither mice nor men
This is the rest of my life
Waiting another lifetime
Before I can live again.

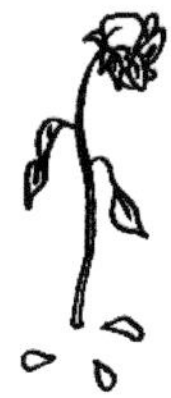

DON'T MESS WITH JULIET

She's stood upright
In the dark
With her arms stretched out
Wide

Don't mess with Juliet
"God's treasures are buried
In broken hearts"

Her story is one of sore, grazed elbows
And tattered, worn, expertly fitted clothes
She knows all the bus times
By heart

Her eyes shine a glance of the Roman empire
Under black, Visigoth sky

Don't mess with Juliet
"God's treasures are buried
In broken hearts"

Her hidden fears multiply and grow
No matter how the dice is thrown
All her dreams end in waking
Or in disappointment.

Her eyes are Eric Stoltz
As Marty McFly

A meticulous genius, weighing up cons and pros
Of looking back at photos
Of when she

Was much better-off.

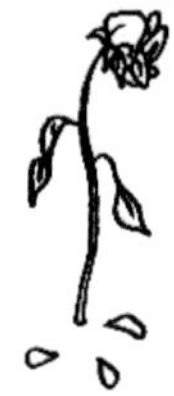

Her arms flail the way the music flows
It saunters and wanders, wherever it chooses to go
All her days are subtitled sighs
But at night, she is alive.

Dancing with her hips
Beaming with joy
With her arms stretched out

Beaming with her hips
Dancing with joy
She's stood, straight upright
In the dark.

LUCKY, LUCKY 7

Several days into November
Here stoked the stroke of the final cut
Music a torment
A teasing, ringing of mockery
Words to mangle the English language
Born ready, but not anymore.

Far too tired to be spiteful, anymore
Death by means of living in November
A little too dizzy for coherent language
Nailed down to the floor, and cut
Well-spoken by mirrors and mirrored means of mockery
Teabag still unopened. Windowsill torment.

The sky ordered a night not so bright, tickled with torment
Such forsaken shadows gone forever, not in sight anymore
The room shakes with gloom and fear, moaned with mockery
For this next week of November
Skirting boards aligned with a tainted cut
Spurred and spurted by mindless language.

Kicked while falling, through most hurtful language
And crestfallen through daily torment
A smile, from the story was cut
Not to be seen, anymore
It was stolen, sold and last shown in November
The hazy lines of paranoia and truth, such blurred mockery.

To sing loudly is to understand mockery
To understand pragmatics, semantics and language
Every emotion in the world, always November
Yes. Yes. Yes. Ear-splitting, screeching torment

Blood-free days dried. No more! No more! Anymore
Clean hands can still be cut.

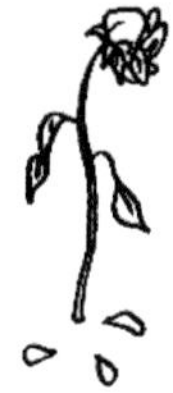

I am only dreamy scenes, now cut
And rolled up sleeves, a mockery
Not to be seen, known or loved anymore
Cloudy, grimacing sky matched with parting language
Ashes lost in a firework, robed in red and green torment
Seven nights into November.

Born ready, but not anymore
There stoked the stroke of the final cut.

Seven days into November
A constant ringing sound of mockery.

Words to mangle the English language
Music a torment.

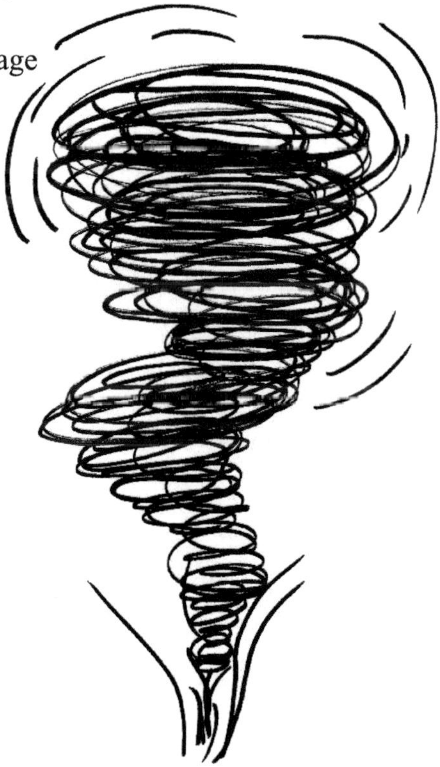

Darkness is easy on the eyes
But heavy on the soul
I have lived on both sides
Of the die
Here I am; appalling
In the clutches of contentment
Someone, anyone… you, please
Tease some humanity out of me

Once you hang up
Your voice shall be forever gone
I am left
Sinking to skinny knees, asking
If I'll ever wake
Again, in April 2019
Or even
Just tomorrow.
In sitting rain
Don't hang up
I'll never hear
Your voice again

Looking for people I've
Never met before in my life
The dreams won't stop
The days won't suffice
Don't hang up
You don't know how long
I have waited for your call
I have wasted away for
You to solve it all

DIVORCE

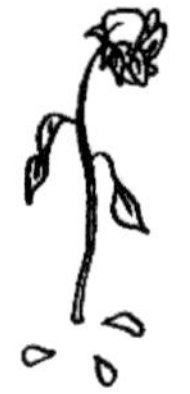

We were the flag at the top of the mountain
Today I have found absolute haplessness and despair
We were the flag at the top of the mountain
I had no idea who I was when I was there
And that was wonderful.
We ruffled all the right feathers
Today, 'one day', 'soon' and 'hopefully'
Have become, 'never'

There are so many happy people
But I don't tend
To spend time with them
If I can be replaced, then
I surely will.

There are so many beautiful things
But I don't know if I want to know
If I can be disgraced, then
Surely, I will be.

We were the flag at the top of the mountain
The branch on the top of the tree
If I can be replaced, then
Surely, I will be.

I can be very easily replaced
I've guessed right again, haven't I?
Surely, I will be.

THE PEOPLE I SEE IN MY DREAMS PT.2

James McKenna! James McKenna! James McKenna!
Who in this hell is James McKenna?

The people I see in my dreams
Have let go of the grip of their hands from me
Soulless body pushed around by the sea
By remorseless, relentless life
Cold harsh steel, yet gentle knife

The people I see in my dreams
Packed away
To wherever, wherever, wherever
Gifts and warnings, are wrapped identically

The people that know they are my dreams
No longer a smile or word for me
Human corpse hung by the quay
Taken away from me

I swear I wanted to break down and cry
And hug your knees
At your visage I envisaged
The person I saw in my dream
Symbol of absolute loss
Dressed in obtuse light blue
I am absolutely rotten and sick
To see scowl, the unforgettable face of you

Too ill to contemplate what this means
The person I saw in my dream
Anything louder than a whisper
Will knock me over
Where once joyous cries the summer day would allow
The winter night, I am so lonely now

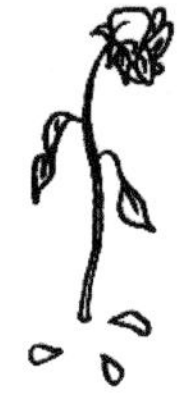

I chased you down from scene to scream
The person I saw in my dream
Only for you to say
You had no use for me tomorrow or today
Stone cold face
In absence of a loving one, impossible to replace

I'm splitting in half
For a certain future, I certainly no longer have
The person I now only see in my dreams

You've walked away from me.

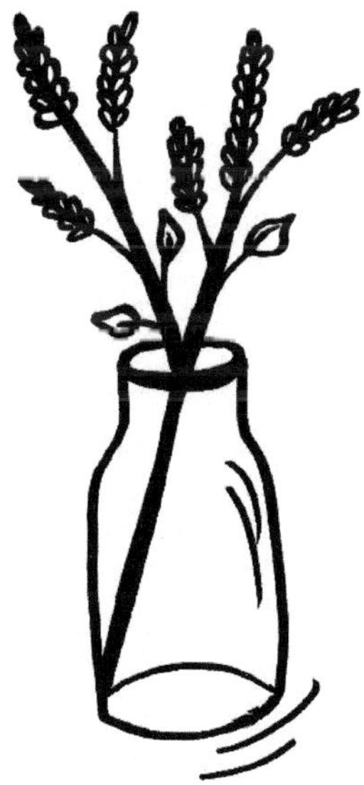

RED RING

I dreamt last night of
The last time we will ever meet
I saw again, holding hands, the marriage of pain and love
I fell, failed, and inhaled
The blended scent of cigarettes and home.

I tried to impress
With my simple smiles, simple stances and
Simple steps
But I fell face down, failed and inhaled
The blended scent of cigarettes and of hope
Painful, crushed hope.

But, Jesus. That walk.
Memory Lane, the only thoroughfare that can attack
Enough to make The Proclaimers
Give up and walk back.

But Jesus. That devil's blessed walk.
Past towering houses, winding paths
And thick black smoke
Of lucid regret, dreaming an aftermath.

But Jesus. That long, slippery walk
Explaining the route with a smile on my face
Tears streaming, stealing my mind
We soon arrived at that place…

Decorated entirely with balloons and well wishers
Of my story, I'm not sure who I had to convince
My chest a convex to distress when I arrived
And it hasn't stopped since

It's much more fun, but hurts much more
To serenade the absent, in a lethargic, soul-destroying trance
I dreamt last night of
The last time, we should dance…

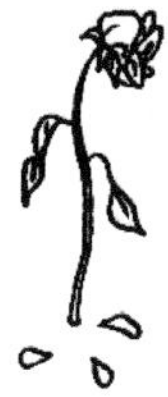

I dreamt last night of
The last time we will ever meet
I fell face down, failed and inhaled
The blended scent of cigarettes and of hope
I'll see you soon, on the 28th June
In an Ethiopian calendar.

I dreamt last night of
The last time, we should dance
At least the boy in my dream
Had that chance.

"Red ring, for what I don't have
Red ring, buried in dreams
Red ring! Red ring! Red ring!
For '*The Things They've Never Seen*'

Red ring! Red ring! Red ring!
It doesn't mean
Anything.

I dreamt, I dreamt
Of red ring.
Please help me.
I don't mean
Anything

Red ring! Red red red red red red
Red red red ring!"

TO BE IN A GARDEN

Oh, to be in a garden
With Mrs. Bardon
Water features spray the lawn and
Our thoughts on the day are far from torn and
I feel alive.

Oh, to be in a garden
With Mrs. Bardon
Summer drips on your forehead in lovely flurries and
The taste of lemonade saps up our worries and
I feel loved.

Oh, to be in a garden
With Mrs. Bardon
Time is ours, we are the silent moon
On a sunny, Sunday afternoon
We will shine when, it is our time to.

Oh, to be in a garden
With Mrs. Bardon
It is now a September evening; we can fight off winter and
Let the flicker of a fire embrace us; let it linger and
I feel warm.

Oh, to be in a garden
With Mrs. Bardon
Smiling and shining and hanging and swaying and
With the sun and moon teasingly playing,
I feel awake.

Oh, to be in a garden
With Mrs. Bardon

We are dreaming, yes, I know
It is undoubtably marvellous here, though
Is it not worth finding a place in reality, we can go?

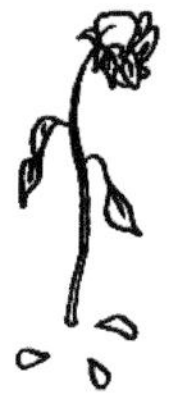

Oh, to be in a garden
With Mrs. Bardon
I am dreaming, yes, I'm aware
Of this idyllic recluse, that we share
But why doesn't reality have just one happy day, it can spare?

We both know one of us is dreaming
But who?
Sadness paves the way; this will all end soon.
One of us shall be destroyed, the other oblivious
Fate and time have no tendencies to be chivalrous

My dreams are often of you
My dreams are bendable, flexible
Unachievable, unacceptable
Of dystopian lands, which are oddly better
Like a crisp ring binder, filled with rejection letters

Oh, to be in a garden
With Mrs. Bardon
But as soon as my adolescent head, hit the pillow
And at 4:18am, I woke
I'm afraid reality, didn't want to know.

SUMMER, CIGARETTE SMOKE

Picturesque, moody dusk
Sets in, and clinches with my skin
Embraced, brazen twilight; life's dancing jewels tend to slowly rust
In front of your eyes, tearful ambiance pulled within

Summer, cigarette smoke
Rises highest, and sends me on edge
It recalls what I remember, how I felt, what I know
The last drips of daylight hang to the sinking window ledge

Window of opportunity slammed shut. It has been closed since when
I first looked in the mirror and saw a spinning, drunken man
Patrolling in his bibulous mind, strolling past where and when
His romance with sentiment began

Lovely, lovely lovely, lovely dusk, take me in your arms
Make it all stop whirling and make it all pleasing
Lovely dusk with passive wistful charms
Too dark to be day, too light to be evening

You know, it doesn't bother me anymore
How often my heart sinks, and rattles on the wooden floor
You know, it doesn't bother me one bit
Which way the wind blows this or that wretched misfit
But,
If only you could see me now
If only you could see me cry now
If only, if only.
Beaten up, black and blue,
In summer, cigarette smoke
I'd still smile for you
If only, if only, if only.

GENTLE KNIFE

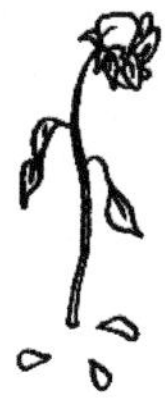

Gentle knife be mine again
Find an incision to cut pouring rain
Gentle knife be kind again
Match blood to sadness, and stings to shame.

Pleasant time break me again
Leave a note so I never forget
Pleasant time kill me again
Scratch lines of loneliness, dressed with regret

Gentle knife be mine again
Find an incision to cut pouring rain
Gentle knife be kind again
Match blood to sadness, and stings to shame.

DEAR FRIEND IN A HOSPITAL BED

I am nothing but dying thoughts of you and
Your absence like rain pouring, with a mould to fit to
I am nothing but cold insincere smiles, a
Wonder, after all that has gone, what is next to do?

I am nothing but November, less days than
Nights, many waving politely aside goodbye road
I am nothing but similar cursed verses
In quest of any place to belong - a comfort, home

Dear friend in a hospital bed
It was the unbridled joy sound of a homecoming
It was the clingy sound of my own funeral
Don't forget

Dear friend in a hospital bed
It was bigger than words, louder than '*Swords*'
Make tomorrow scream louder than all gone before
Don't forget

Dear friend in a hospital bed
Don't ask me what I expected -
It wasn't this
Don't forget, don't forget, don't forget

You are nothing but dying thoughts of me and
My spark, just like the extreme thrill of the pouring rain
You are nothing but tired, limping half miles and
A tension headache of joyous, screaming triumphant pain

You are nothing but all and everything I have
Nicely fitting trousers and internet browsers
Evenings by the silent dog and bone, and
The art of dying alone.
Don't forget.

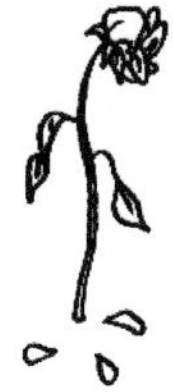

Dear friend in a hospital bed,
It was bigger than words, louder than *'Swords'*
Make tomorrow scream louder than all gone before
Don't forget.

NEW BOOK

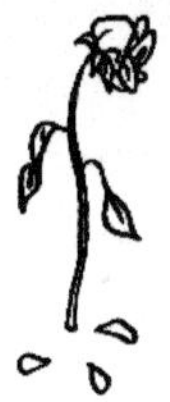

So, he stood there
Presenting the collection of pages,
With all of the valour of a poet
Bestowing his very own heart.

His grin shone with such a glow
It lit up the whole room around them.
His figure cast a giddy shadow
Toes and knees dancing with sheer excitement,
Patrolling through each page one by one,
Searching for a line to regurgitate to his friend
In order to receive a sense of validation for his true love that
Sat in his hands.

TOASTER

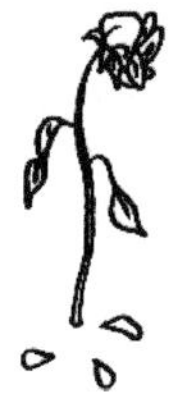

I did an experiment with the toaster
I turned the dial upon each new insertion
And upon each careful turn
I am now glad to have learnt
The bread becomes
Ever so slightly more burnt

I did an experiment with the toaster
Where is the limit of its charms?
It battled bread, flat breads, and bagels
And even the bread with strange looking fruit
Of unconcealed joy
I was no longer in pursuit

I did an experiment with the toaster
I put it in the bath
I was lifted, and away you went
I was tormented
No longer.

HOW AM I FEELING?

How am I feeling?
I'm feeling everything
The birds,
The trees
And the gentle Yorkshire breeze.

How am I feeling?
I'm feeling everything
The pleasant morning,
The shouts and waves from across the road
And the sadness I am (somehow) still owed.

How am I feeling?
I'm feeling everything
I'm feeling incredibly lost
I feel the lament of my threadbare arms
I feel the effect of regret, without charm.

How am I feeling?
I'm feeling everything
All is in slow motion
Time will not move past
All is in slow motion, yet devastatingly fast.

How am I feeling?
I'm feeling everything
I feel lyrics and poems
Reeling through my mind
I feel given up on and
Brushed aside. "Bye bye!"

How am I feeling?

I'm feeling everything
I am crushed,
Confused,
Uncontrollably cunningly mused

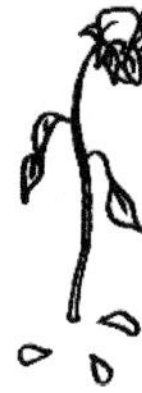

How am I feeling?
I'm feeling everything
I am burning,
I'm drowning,
Permanently frowning

How am I feeling?
I'm feeling everything
I am squashed
And rocked
'Seasick, yet still docked'

How am I feeling?
I simply cannot move.
How am I feeling?
I'm feeling everything
I'm feeling the closing words to my eulogy
Distress has run free
I'm feeling all the words
You ever said to me.

LEAVING HIGH ROAD

Don't wander too far away from me
As much as your mind wishes to try
What is left of dusk and tangerine mortality?
"Let's part whilst
We can still say goodbye"

Don't stop to wonder what might have been
Please God, stop me from stopping to cry
What is left of streetlights and belle aujourd'hui?
"Let's go before
We grow old and die"

November, don't you love me?
Leaving High Road
All is seen at its best
In the dark
To be real is a precious, valuable thing
Not one word wasted
Or left unknown
Leaving High Road

My heart bleeds inside my body
At the sound of your compassion
My workmanship is for all to see, though it is shoddy
And in the cymbal rain, seems devoid of all passion

Tommy became aware of his own existence, he walked in such a daze
He was never able to act or speak again
He married his wife's brother, he sawed off both of his legs
I only cut off one of mine
Left uncrossed and lost
Distinguished by the lingering, yearning scent

Of absence

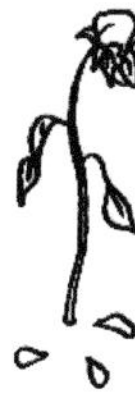

What emancipates tied hands, I am without
Though my heart is far from withdrawn
It is only June, but before the year is out
This will all be gone

Your presence is like ashes, like dust
And all that cannot be touched
I'm so decent that I'm almost dead
Leaving High Road
Yes, yes, yes. No.
Not one single second spared
Or left unknown
Leaving High Road.

I AM, JUST I

Strength and honesty in walking legs
Magnitude, relief in breath

Careful, meticulous nature of special hands
The soul packed punch of the right glance

Smooth crisp silken jacket, baring unconditional love
Crushing morals, fables we pretend dwell above

Life in trees, shushing lullaby of wind
Lurking, hopeless chance of tomorrow to rescind

Desire and magnetism, will always outlive satisfaction
Of brutal, unsustainable, inexplicable attraction

Alluring wordless poetry of careful, resolute hair
Charged with warning notions of 'ignorance beware'

Time's whine to turn the oranges to black
Time's chime to slowly put everything back, where it was

Such crying connection to what is years or seconds gone
Harassment of the mind to fit, and to belong

Strength and pride lay in content standing legs
Relief and hope in miserly breath

To believe you are just you
Or I, am just I
Is such a fatal lie.

YOU WERE THE LION TAMER

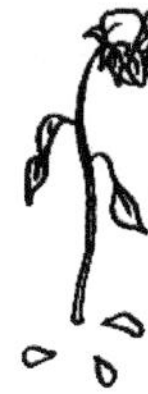

I'll slink around the edges,
Like a gloomy cat in the halls.
If I am to stay
Will you patiently watch the way?
I shrink on the pages,
In deep red, like passion and blood.

Possibly, maybe, definitely going mad
What doesn't kill you, makes you wish it had.
With the seasons,
Desire sways and changes.

I'll roll around the ages
Like a miserable mountaineer in Nepal
Run the hamster wheel
And whirl a dubious deal
Here I am, here I am.

You'll find me breaking the rules
Of whatever it is you humans do
I am to brush past the guilt-edged fleece of sorrow
And, to fall asleep in the arms of tomorrow.

BROKEN, GLUM SON

I say none of these dreadful words in jest
The father screamed in disgust at his new-born son, in ear-piercing distress.
There was no remedy or therapy to suggest,
For the boy born a distorted, mangled mess.

As years passed by like flying pages in a windy town
Whenever the boy would gaze around, broken and glum
The dad would kneel down
Next to the gasping, voiceless son
"Please do not worry, not today, not
Tomorrow, not ever
When we smile, the rest of the world stops
When we are here, and we're together
Nothing in the world can be wrong
Nothing could possibly be wrong"

Happy time went past
For the father and the son.
But for reasons nobody dare ask,
In the surrounding towns, war pressed on.

The dad cried
As the dreadful son gasped,
And then knowingly sighed,
As the sun came out, alas
At 11 o'clock at night; the sun shone disconcertingly bright
At 11 o'clock at night.

The dad looked at the sky, at the hazy, fuzzy white
Tortuous event, and opened his mouth to shout,
Whilst the son marvelled at the oncoming sight

As the sun came out
At 11 o'clock at night.

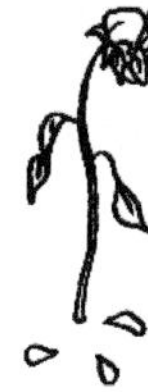

I say none of these dreadful words in jest
But the son felt alive for the very first time
As his sliced and divided body set with the sun in the west
The sweet scent of extinction lingered, like coffee and lime

As the sun came out
At 11 o'clock at night.

RESTING WITH INK

Steadily kick the hands
Around the clock
Whether you slip with passion
Or you do not
Caress the minutes along
Twist the mind, perplexed
Poised with pen
Tick-tock. Tick-tock.
Address each distress

Limp along in
Flip-flop times
Where the life in each day
Is to tell what is felt
In stories, through a rip of the page
Stop the flight in the night
Disengage
Skies fall in simple ways
Enslaved by creativity, shadows and rain

Be remembered as
Certainty in solitude
A validation of loneliness
Fit quite amicably, quite magically
In ill-fitted jeans
Draft a steady plan
Meticulous meaning behind grieving
By now, you know the truth
And what it all means

Let each corner of the page
Either sold or stole

Ignite the soul
Allow each mirror of what is lost
To remain, with inky cost
Tick-tock. Tick-tock.
Steadily, arise and formulate
Disputes and flukes are nestled here always
Simply spewing out the couplets, of these torrid days

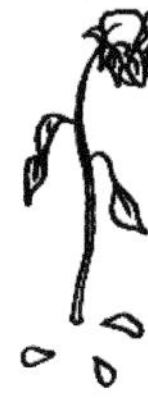

Meet the other ones, so bold
Fawningly courageous
Such sickly ironic gold-edged pages
The words they speak
Such humbling defeat
Never never never
Match the shoes on their feet
Why be one with this cry of spurious sentiment?
To see the only outlet, all you have
Neglected to the elements

Darkness has dissolved into despair
Mundane has bled into bleak
See the hills clasp the rain
Feel the elegiac buzz, once again
Pay your bills for
Your backhanded gifts
Give the earth your most unsubtle body,
Be you.
You, who shall not be named
The shine of sun, on lonely days

The thrilling sense of permanence
That rests within the resting ink
Sits there, to make you stop
To bring you back to the brink
Fiery spark inside, ripping through skin

To come out and scream.
Without the ungainly words on show
Of all people, I should know
The saviour from insanity respites between the lines
Scripted and sculptured
To save the whines behind the blinds

Where we shall lay, this dusty shelf
The mannerisms will always match so delicately
Please now prepare yourself
For all I am
Your memories of me.

IT FEELS LIKE YESTERDAY

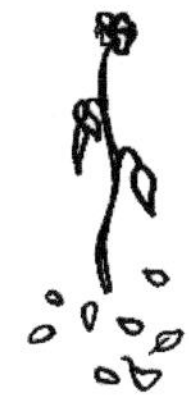

I am 55 days without alcohol
It feels like yesterday
It feels like yesterday
I am 70 days without your call
It feels like yesterday

I am 29 hours wrapped in a cocoon
And I don't know what to do
I am 10 minutes without you
I haven't got a couplet or a clue

I am 6 seconds without a thought of suicide
It feels like now is the time
To run and to hide
My posture is both tried and tired
Tell me how and why and why and how.

I am the gone-off salad dressing of yesterday
(Better unexplained)
I am charging head first into infamous fame
In such pain

I am 2 small years without a smothering, marshmallow coat
It feels like yesterday
It feels like yesterday
And 12 minutes from a knife at my throat
It could only be today
It must be, today.

I am 30 seconds without alcohol
It feels like yesterday
It feels like yesterday
I am 15 years without your call
It feels like yesterday.

MOTHER WITH HER ARMS CROSSED

Mother, with her arms crossed and as it
Is half past twenty-five, she can recall what she knows
You never did have
The fingers for piano.

Mother with her arms crossed surely, she can start
To live amongst us, after so long in a shallow oval
She's a little unhappy
But aren't we all?

Mother, with her arms crossed
A Lazarus sign for fears still very much alive
Picture a river so incessantly tedious
Why not take a dive?

Mother, with her arms firmly crossed
What will end, will end
Heartless, but so full of love
What will end, will end.

STAR OF STAGE

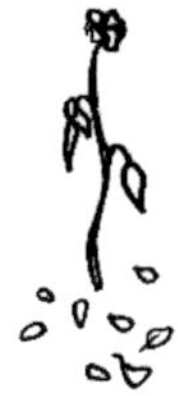

A young boy approached me,
And told me how he was utterly fascinated by the play.

The lights, the stage, the sentiment...
I could see the awe ooze from his soul, and glimmer in his eyes.

Naturally, a suicide attempt was what followed for the admiring child,
And I'm not sure exactly what else he expected.

I think age has absolutely nothing to do with naivety.
I see many people in the dying embers of age
Who stroll around without a care or desire in the universe
Surely it is not experience,
Which has taught them such ease in the world?
This just can't be the case.
Your age has absolutely no correlation whatsoever with how long your life has been.
I have certainly lived a thousand times already.

LEARNING TO SPELL FLUORESCENT

Learning to spell fluorescent
Will become so clear, you'll see
When you learn the letters
Roll off the tongue
So delightfully, so easily

F-L-U
O-R-E
S-C-E-N-T

Learning to spell fluorescent
There's no need for fuss or fear
As in your mind
You will find
The letters simply appear

F-L-U
O-R-E
S-C-E-N-T

Learning to live in silence
In company with pouring rain
Becomes no worry
As, in a hurry
You can whisper the rhyme again

F-L-O
U-U-O
S-E-N-T

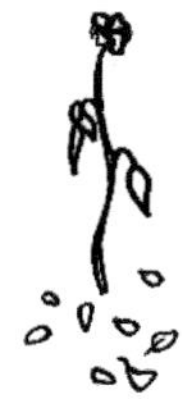

Learning to laugh
At this utter mess
Becomes pleasant with time
All is happy and fine
For these letters spell success

F-F-F
U-R-E
C-C-C-C-C

Learning to
Could divide us and them
And yes ----
But, yes of course
Here it is again!

D-I-E
S-L-O
E-R

Squint through
18 years
It is
Not enough

F-L-E
"Do not screech
As I slit your throat"
T-T-T-T
"Again
They cannot hear your
Brain SCREAM
A-A-F-L-A-A-A"

Learning to spell
Learning to flooresent
So delightfully!
So easily!

Radio silence
Radio silence
Radio silence
F-L-U
O-R-E
Radio silence

Radio silence

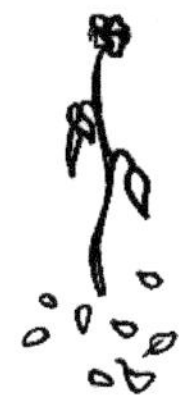

Sit on
The hillside
Be rocked
Be mocked
See how
Wolf white-blue
Human eagle eyes
Pierce through you

Sit on
The hillside
Be rocked
Be mocked
To dizziness
Is it delusion?
Or cruel irony?
Are they staring back at you?
Or smiling back at me?

Radio silence
Radio silence
Radio silence
And yes ----
Radio silence

PANDORA'S BOX

"I have never believed
In the supernatural
However, in this situation
From the idea - it is difficult to be free
A giant purple creature in the sky
Pressing buttons to form my demise

Such pertinent mental, physical torture
Comes packaged, shaped around the reality
I find myself trapped in
The tremendous black and white film
Which sleep lends to me
Is only formed to punish, internally

I give unbridled thanks
To my subconscious
For that little intricacy
How the specifics often waver
Is not for me to say
But, Pandora's box is built this way…

We sit in the crowded common room
Laid in the sweaty hands of gloom
A familiar scene
The garishly vile decoration of faded orange seats
And graffiti tattered walls
Stand even more nauseating, in the pit
Of tedious immortality
I stand with Vivian
In a relatively enclosed space
Her hair, a trivial but mesmerising mess
It is easy, to call familiarly safety

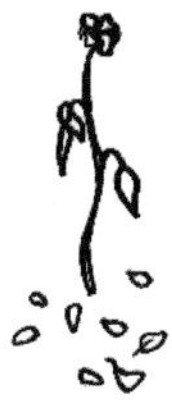

Though, I am experienced enough in eerie nights
To know it is suspicion

My soul folds
Like a hopeful young girl
Alone, waiting by the telephone
Soon to be frozen
And eaten by time
Utterly absorbed by
Loneliness, a very best friend
Remembering each word that was ever said
Each word never said
In a maze of despair
A maze of mist
A smoggy suffocating loss

With only the warning
Of yesterday's terror
The lights are cut out
As quickly as an unexpected heartbreak
Leaving no trace that I
Or anyone around
Was ever there to begin with
Screams are heard
From mouths untried in this hellish home
I am fully aware of the striking blow
Which is to follow

The strike in question
Is that of a dreary, teal coloured
Double decker bus
It stands, with headlights
Tangerine eyes watching, waiting
In the dark
The four-wheeled stench of home

Stands a considerable distance from me
Driverless, merciless
Entirely magnanimous
In the face of its impending victory
In an act of twisted revenge
It's head tips towards mine
In heavy, lingering robustly determined dread
My feet are tied

The way in which the inside lights
Illuminate with fear the November-esque darkness
Resembles the heart closing violins
Falling backwards, whilst totally blind
It resembles every night I remember so well
But have been forced by time
To leave behind"

MAN ALIVE

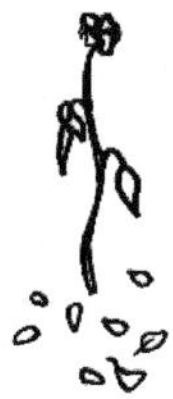

Days longer
Teeth sharper
Death by
Mutual consent
Man alive.

I moved out
Yesterday and
Hello.
Now I am
Back again
Man alive.

People don't change
And
Unfortunately
Nor do I
Man alive.

Remembering
Before the blanket fell
Even then
It wasn't alright
Man alive.

August is November
September is August
September is September
Every night is November.
Making mistakes
I didn't even understand
At the time
Man alive.

THE OTHER SIDE OF THE LAKE

The other side of the lake
Folded corner of an abandoned

Page
Unreturned to
The other side of the lake,
What we are is
Certainly not what we knew.

The true colours of the rainbow
Are impossible to change

On the
Other side of the lake,
Step-cousin's wellington boot, half removed,
Slant of the autumn, angled towards you.
The other side of the lake,
Sadness rhymes, but numbness
Simply doesn't.

Place my eyes on light's shelf
As my mind analyses
That I still have myself
Whoever that is.

The true colours of the rainbow

As I stop and think
And I casually throw the stone
At the perfect angle to the glossy, lucid-less sea
Will it again, bounce back and slap me?

The other side of the lake.
I half-smile,
I don't know why,
The other side of the lake.
I have smiled
But I, don't know why

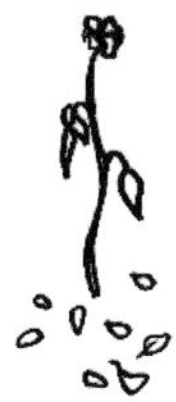

As seen from
As seen from
I'll see you from
The other side of the lake.
I'll see you from
The other side of the lake.
What we are is
Certainly not what we knew

BEFORE IT GETS LIGHT AGAIN

It's best not to dwell
On being alive and well
I will give my life to the letter Y
And I will fly to Bahrain
Before it gets light again
Before it gets light again

I didn't, I don't have a clue
With an expression like June's full moon
And a face like a popped balloon
I don't know why I love you
But I do
It was a sonnet
For a Wednesday afternoon

Daisy pin badge, never bought
Left for a battle unfought
As quick as summer comes, it goes
And we said cheerio
We said goodbye
For how long, who knows?

I don't take any pleasure
Or reward, an unequal measure
In always being right
Out went the light, it was night
And so, we said goodbye
And so, we said goodbye

Daisy pin badge, so sublime
It takes all my time
To look after myself

I will poison myself in the name of good health
Before it gets light again
Before it gets light again

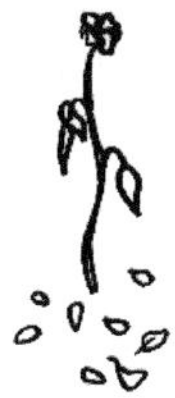

It's best not to dwell
On being alive and well
Always heading the opposite way, and yet still here
For heaven's sake, just disappear
I'll be on my way to hell and pain
Before it gets light again
Before it gets light again

THE PUB ACROSS FROM THE RBS

I am a broken, burnt, fallen tree
You'll change your mind, around half past three
And you'll say "meet me"
Time? Date? Too late,
Too late.

As very often you
Are the exception to the rule
Would you like to hear the story I tell people?
Or the one that is true?
Now silence, once silver blue
'Lucretia, my reflection'
Too late,
So, so late.

I too have been hurt
And worn as smile as if it were a stain on your shirt
So, say you will stay
And stand by my side
You are the most wonderful person
I have met in my life.

I'm dizzy from all the spinning around
All the small talk
All the sentiments whispered in chalk
I'm waiting for the happiest days
Of my life.

Another year skips by
I'm not sure anyone knows how, or why

All I know is
You are the most wonderful person
I have met in my life.

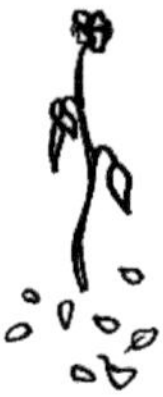

LATVIAN STRANGERS

Latvian strangers
You came and you saw
More of my mind
Than there is to explore

I politely waved hello and you said,
"The nightlife in this town
Is drawing its last breath"
And proceeded to point out
All of our impending deaths
Latvian strangers
You came and you saw

Latvian strangers
You leave behind
More confusion than is palatable
For all of mankind

I found you a broken wreck and you said,
"I'd give up on suicide
But God loves a trier"
And then you proceeded to set
Your strawberry-blonde hair on fire
Latvian strangers
You leave behind

Latvian strangers
You came and you saw
More dismembered limbs
Than in the second World War

You found my own mind and it said,

"I can be incredibly creative at finding positives
I just tend not to use that superpower"
I'll explain the meaning of life
If you give me a quarter of an hour
Latvian strangers
Leave me alone

Latvian strangers
You came and you saw
More of my heart
Than I knew was yours

I pinned you down and you said,
"In this world
I have absolutely nothing"
And then you proceeded to steal
All of my shopping
Latvian strangers
You came and you saw

I tracked you down and you said,
"You're a twisted
Spiteful wreck"
I said, "I see where you're coming from
At least, the chunk of me that's left"
Latvian strangers
Are all that can be adored

Latvian strangers
You leave nothing but a taste
Of all that can be adored.

PLEASE, NO MORE

Every time, I am not
The face to be adored
I am so alone
So
Please, no more

Lord only knows
The dark nights
Decorated before me

All I have to give
Is to fall asleep

New horizons
Aren't anywhere near
As bright as they sound
Memories anchor my soul
I see them around

Wind wandering through swaying trees
Is this the only company left with me?
No one in sight
For ten thousand miles

Silence is the only voice
I can acknowledge, and reply goodbye
No one around, with a thought to spare
For the man still a child

I have been there, with arms open wide
All of those days, all of this time
Why now, are there no one's arms stretched out

To comfort mine?
Please, no more.

These are, by far
The darkest days
Of my life

All I have to give
Is to give up
And die.

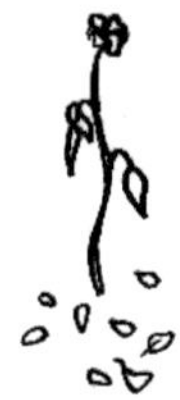

BUS STOP

Bus, stop. I'm dying.
Please, stop. It hurts too much.
Bus, stop. Before it returns.

Bus, stop.
I want to get off.

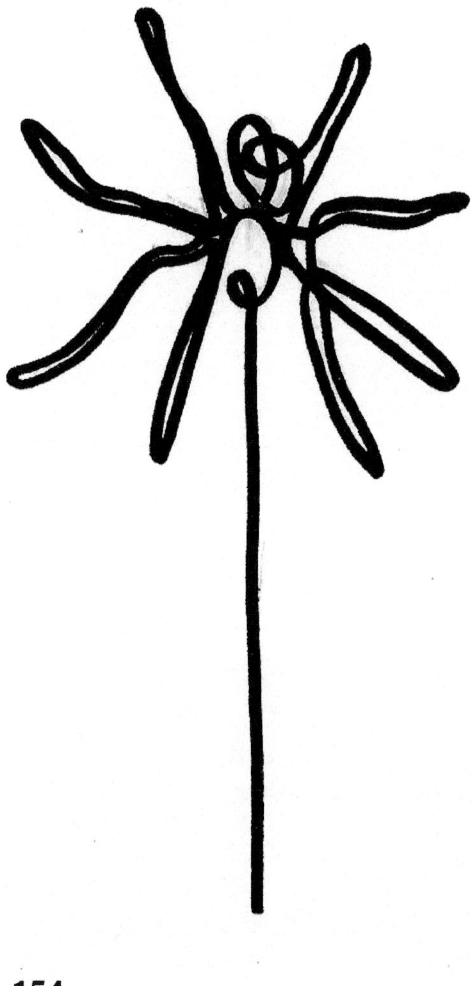

THE LONG ROAD BACK PT.2

'The Long Road Back' original poem can be found in 'The Things They've Never Seen'.

The long road back, from spiritual awakening
I have nowhere to turn, on these cold winter evenings
Your electricity and warmth, nowhere to be seen
Unhappy, by all means.

Instead glancing over at him or her
There is no substitute for what has been lost, I am absolutely sure
The dreams won't stop. I cannot wake and smile, I must concur
I do not have that luxury, anymore.

The way my solitude drowns in the night
I am blinded by darkness, once again
The sheer art of absence, flowers that were white
As I walk home, it begins to rain.

The long road back, from spiritual awakening
I have nowhere to turn, on such cold winter evenings.

MY FRIENDS

My friends,
You are both the start
And the end
Of my words and my heart,
Shot down in its grinning prime
The first time
Only happens once
And stings, for months and months
Flung into outer space.
Slice at the throat, with a knife so blunt
I know my place.

If anyone, unlike myself,
With a solid grip of reality
And a place on the shelf
Would care to explain all of this to me
That would be very kind.
Because, I promise I have tried,
But days only make sense and belong
Once they've shifted along.
And when they're finally over and done
And long gone
I know my place, dazzled by the sun

Nostalgia is blinding.
Nights are only recognisable
Upon emergency crash landing.
Action as a result of thought
Far from advisable
Shot down by eye rhyme.
The last time
Happens, and flies away.

Every. Single. Day.
I lost my only ace
With no more cards left to play
I know my place.

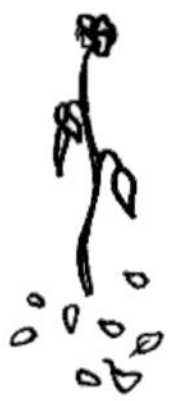

My friends,
Is there any need to explain why and how?
With myself, I am far too tired to make amends
This is only goodbye for now
I was begging, down on my knees
For him to disagree with me.
But no, he must abide
I'll fall asleep, and slide
Taking a familiar step, without trace
Moving aside
I know my place.

My friends,
You are the start and the end
Of the strain in my veins.
So, be happy
Smile, spend and descend.
It's all that remains.

SMILE BY THE CHAPEL

They talk the talk, tomorrow and today
They talk the talk, and then walk away
Smile by the chapel;
Everything will be ok.

Run very fast and chase around the past, optimism slimmer
For heaven's sake stop! Give hope a glimmer,
And remember the hideous monster
You see in in the mirror.

One day, arising through the smoke,
You'll find a sharp-tonged bloke.

I dreamt last night of giant breakthrough;
I saw blessed brown eyes and a midlands hairdo.
Now I wake; I am still the same, having started anew
I pray to have Jesus, the way that you do.

They say what they say, today and tonight
They'll push you given the chance, from any height
Smile by the chapel;
Everything will be alright.

Your crying face was quite becoming
In November pouring rain, sleet and something
I dreamt last night of more than I can say or ask
I saw a comforting smile and soothing grasp.

One day, he'll appear as there's no seconds to spare
Sauntering ominously down the apple and the pears

They talk the talk, tomorrow and today

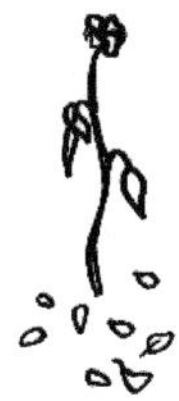

They talk the talk, and then walk away
Smile by the chapel
Everything will be ok.

Your crying face was quite becoming
In November pouring rain, sleet and something

I dreamt last night of giant breakthrough
I saw blessed brown eyes and a midlands hairdo
Now I wake; I am still the same, having started anew
I pray to have Jesus, the way that you do.

I WAS RIGHT

Chevrolet, car cuts through smoke
I arrived as the punchline of the joke
It was all ok and fixed, but then it broke
I was right.

Ryan has got a nasty scar,
Forced sneers and real tears are so bizarre.
He fell and vomited, after he came so far
I was right.

Steel cup, plentiful table,
Is just tomorrow's miss-sold fable.
I promise, I kept going for as long as I was able
I was right.

Now, it's over and done,
Whether or not I was supposed to stay strong.
The last chapter has come, and its gone;
I was right.

I walked to Wakefield, I tried,
I walked to Austria, I cried,
And feared you'd say goodbye.
And
I was right.

February, February,
February coach
Drive me home.
February, February,
February smoke
Lift me home.

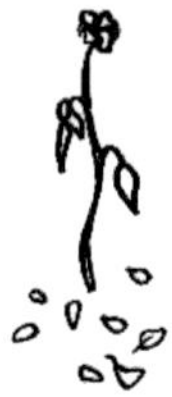

February coach is a reminder
I am nobody's future.
Heart alive and full at Easter
Dead before all of Yorkshire.

February, February
February coach
Teaches me
More than what is necessary;
February, February
February coach
Drive me home.

February, February
February coach
Love me today and
Tomorrow
February, February
Once alone, still alone
Drive me home.

December coach, I arrive home
The profane aisle is not to compare
Yet still
I look into darkness
And hope that somehow, you're there.

I look point blank into the lonely darkness
And I pray to God that you are there,

But I am never right.

ONE THOUSAND WORDS

If people only had one thousand words
How would the world change?
And if living was a paid skill
I'd be below minimum wage.

If people only had one thousand words,
Magnification of the desperation of song,
Would it then be easier to explain
How it's all going wrong?

If people had to think before they spoke,
And roads were costly crossed,
Would you then remember
All I was worth, and all I was?

If people had a limit on the nonsense passed around,
And confinity served as a fatal guide,
My arms, would stay naively
Still stretched out, open wide.

In vino veritas,
And how the truth did gush.
I used one million words in a single night
And how in the morning did I blush.

If I had only three words left to use
I'd still tell you, every time
That I loved you.

JANUARY 1st

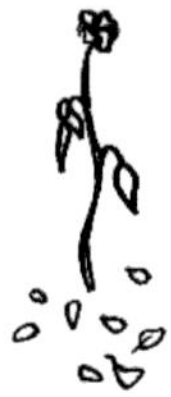

Grief; cold proportions, not from the mourner
But from me, who is to be mourned… and you
Shall call by, tomorrow or soon after
Surely you will forget? You often do.

Day black, night blacker; so, goodnight indeed
One year ago, I was rough, styled and wild
Yet as alive as a scribbling stirred poet
Yet… as comfortable as a treasured child

January first, afraid to love or dream
I am stuck with a losing rule of thumb
I am solo… with all I have ever been
Today, for whatever next is to come

I am stuck with all I have tried to shun
Tomorrow, whatever is next to come.

GOODNIGHT, LOVELY

You've become just a bottom drawer
A memory to be pushed away, on busy days.

Understand November nights and think of me as the sun
I shall not hide on cold Tuesdays.

December 1st, six months today
All will be ok
December 3rd, six months today
All will be ok
December 1st, six months today
All will be ok
December 61st, six million years today
All will be ok

You've become what I cannot ignore
A treasure buried for another's gaze.

You are the opera, the unsteady patio
You are the summer, the *'Pink Bullets'* to amaze.

I persuade myself that, even though the sun is scoldingly bright
This is not goodbye, this is goodnight.

You've become the bedroom floor
A most uncomfortable place to stargaze.

But you know I was a fool
For a pedestal of praise.

December 3rd, six months today
All will be ok.

December 3rd, six months today
All will be ok
December 3rd, six months today
All will be ok
December 3rd, six and a half million years today
How could any of this be, ok?

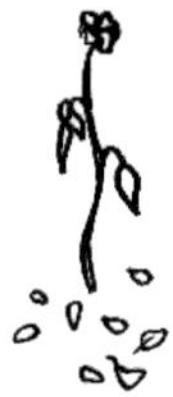

I am walking to the beaming smile of the future
I am running towards the darkness of tomorrow's door.

From tranquil life, to tranquil death
In less than a breath.

I persuade myself that, even though the sun is scoldingly bright
This is not goodbye, this is goodnight.

From tranquil life, to tranquil death
In less than a breath.

I persuade myself that, even though the sun is scoldingly bright
This is not goodbye, this is goodnight.

Goodnight
Goodnight
Goodnight
Goodnight
Goodnight
Goodbye!
Goodbye!

Oh God. Help me.

I WAS A WALNUT TREE

Two years ago,
I was a sweeping, wild expanse of time ahead.
Two years ago,
On February 27th, I waved and smiled, "goodnight",
Time knows, it was to be a galloping, heavy-hearted hello.

Two years ago,
I was a February coach.
Two years ago,
I was Guido Orefice, staring across at you in the mezzanine,
And away from the actors in the show.

Two years ago,
I was the hope of spring, a cloud gliding by my mind.
Two years ago,
I would stay younger than spring,
With the sparkling, flowing, lovely nights to follow.

Two years ago,
I was a February coach,
Tonight, I am alone.
Two years ago,
I was a walnut tree,
With a thousand future moons to follow,
Tonight, what is there but tomorrow?

Two years ago,
I gazed into smog and saw dazzling happy lights,
Tonight, I sit with Klaus Nomi as the dusk weeps goodbye.
Tonight, I sit and ponder the depth of the window pane,
Whilst the sting of life and love has won again.

Two years ago,
I was a walnut tree
With a thousand future happy days to follow me
Tonight, I have only my thoughts
I was a walnut tree.

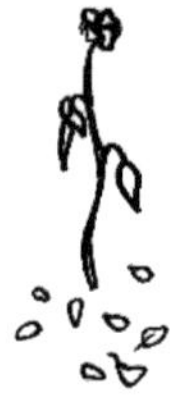

The war goes on
I have surrendered already
I was a walnut tree.

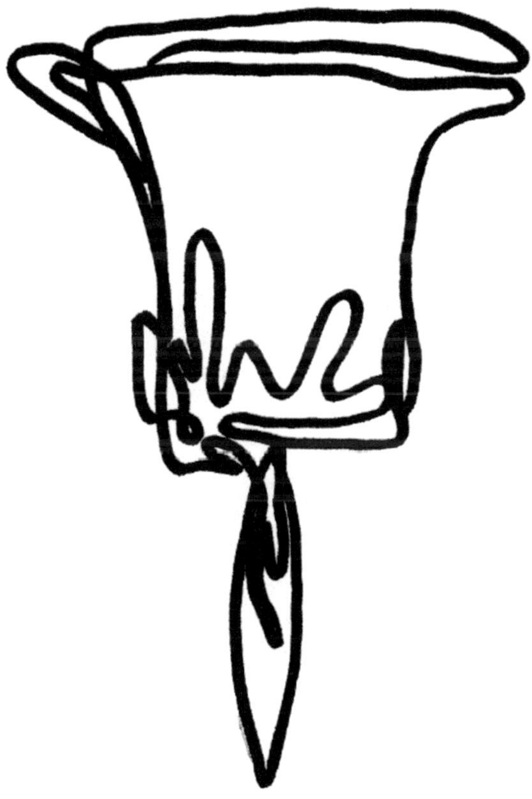

TO THOSE WHO HAVE DEPARTED THIS JOURNEY

For a hapless happening
I'm open wide, a mile
With uncertain hidden smiles
Remembering then.

For a gone buddy
My heart is hurting
And the ruler of regret is asserting
Whatever it can.

For unequivocal solitude
In certainty, without a clue
For the many who
Have departed this journey.

To those who halved and doubled and doubled and halved
All of the mess, trickery and equinox worry
To the many who have departed this journey
I am sorry.

To those who have shifted gears
Follow me and we will not turn back
To the many who have departed this journey
I have no yearning for anger or attack.

To those who left me stranded on the doorstep
Love existed for just a minute, I am sure
To the many who have departed this journey
I have no further thought of you, left to endure.

To those who opened the doors to the last chance saloon
And pointed the direction of where to go
To the many who have departed this journey
Thank you for doing so.

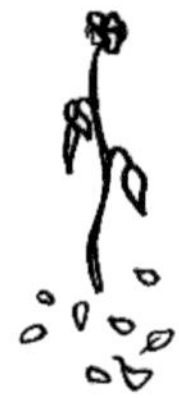

And what or whatever resilience
That is left clinging to my chest
I have no more spare time to invest
In licking wounds, lucid tunes… or shame.

Come and share the middle C with me
Although at one time, it was very nice
I have broken my neck twice
Looking backwards.

Once sighing on a street, crying in estate
Wherever next you or I go
Clearly you still do not know
What you have left behind.
To many who have departed this journey
Thank you for doing so.

END OF SECTION B

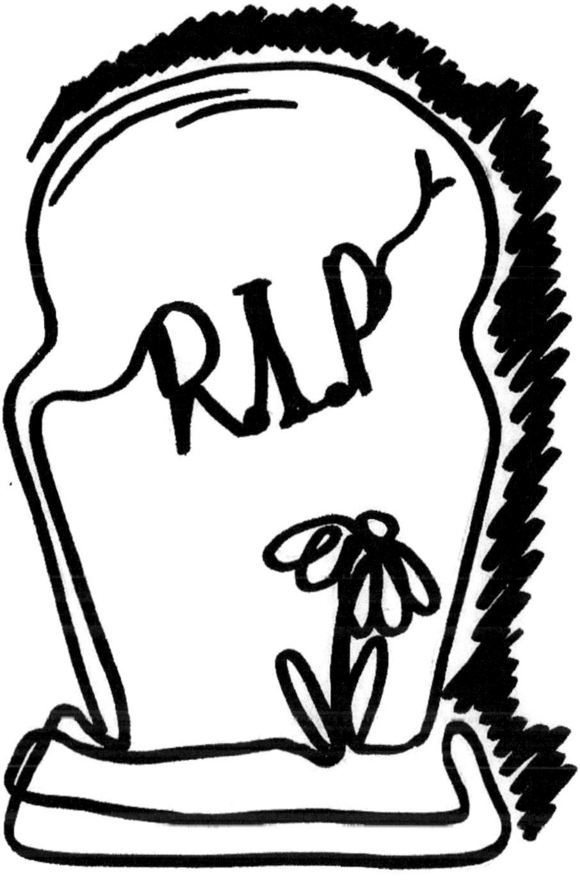
RIP

SO MUCH TO ACKNOWLEDGE…

A huge, heartfelt thanks to all those who made this book possible.
Thanks to BPUK for their support and guidance, for both *'Every Night is November'* and *'The Things They've Never Seen'*.
Thank you to the extremely talented Abi for her illustrations. As I'm sure you will agree, they're absolutely wonderful. She has managed to illustrate what my shaking hands cannot draw, and my shaking mind cannot describe.
Thank you to all the talented musicians who allowed their music to be used for the recorded readings on YouTube, and thank you to Hannah for her contributions and voice recording. I'm very grateful.
A thank you to my ever-critical proof readers, who assured there was never a moment without feeling completely self-conscious about every word I had scrawled.
Thank you to everyone who has thrown advice at me along the way. I am unbelievably proud of '*Every Night is November*'. It is the pinnacle of my work, and I'm sure, the best collection I'll ever write.

The biggest thank you, as so very often, goes to my dad, Paul. Not only my dad, but a support, a photographer, a taxi driver, a proof-reader, a mentor, a role model, an advisor, and above all, my best friend. This is impossible without you, for so many reasons.

Thank you to all who have read. All who have, and will, greet this book with indifference, with hate and with love.

What is next? I'm not so sure. Does it really matter?
"All I do know, is we're here, and it's now"

In certainty, without a clue,
Jacob.

<u>NEVER, EVER FORGET…</u>

PETA (People for the ethical treatment of animals) – www.peta.org.uk

SHELTER – www.shelter.org.uk

MERCY FOR ANIMALS – mercyforanimals.org

GREENPEACE – www.greenpeace.org.uk

MIND - www.mind.org.uk

ABOUT THE AUTHOR

"Born and living in West Yorkshire, England, Jacob Davies has become a poet who can reflect the complexities and struggles of living as a young person in confusing times. His acute wit, clarity and ability to articulate the seemingly incomprehensible, sets him apart whilst creating a rare resonance with his audience that brings to the fore the thoughts many have and try to keep hidden.

His poetry is his way of expressing his views, his anger, his incredulity and his complete lack of comprehension over how the world functions today. His first collection *'The Things They've Never Seen'* accumulated much praise and intrigue from his growing numbers of supporters who continue to appreciate his red raw honesty and openness. *'Every Night is November'* is his second published poetry collection.

Aside from his poetry, Jacob is also co-editor of Morrissey fanzine *'Knockabout World'*, which was founded in 2020 and has released four issues to date. He also has written a number of short stories.

Jacob is a huge music fan and an avid reader, with Anne Sexton, Oscar Wilde, Morrissey, Belle & Sebastian and Mark Morriss cited as his influences in literature and music."

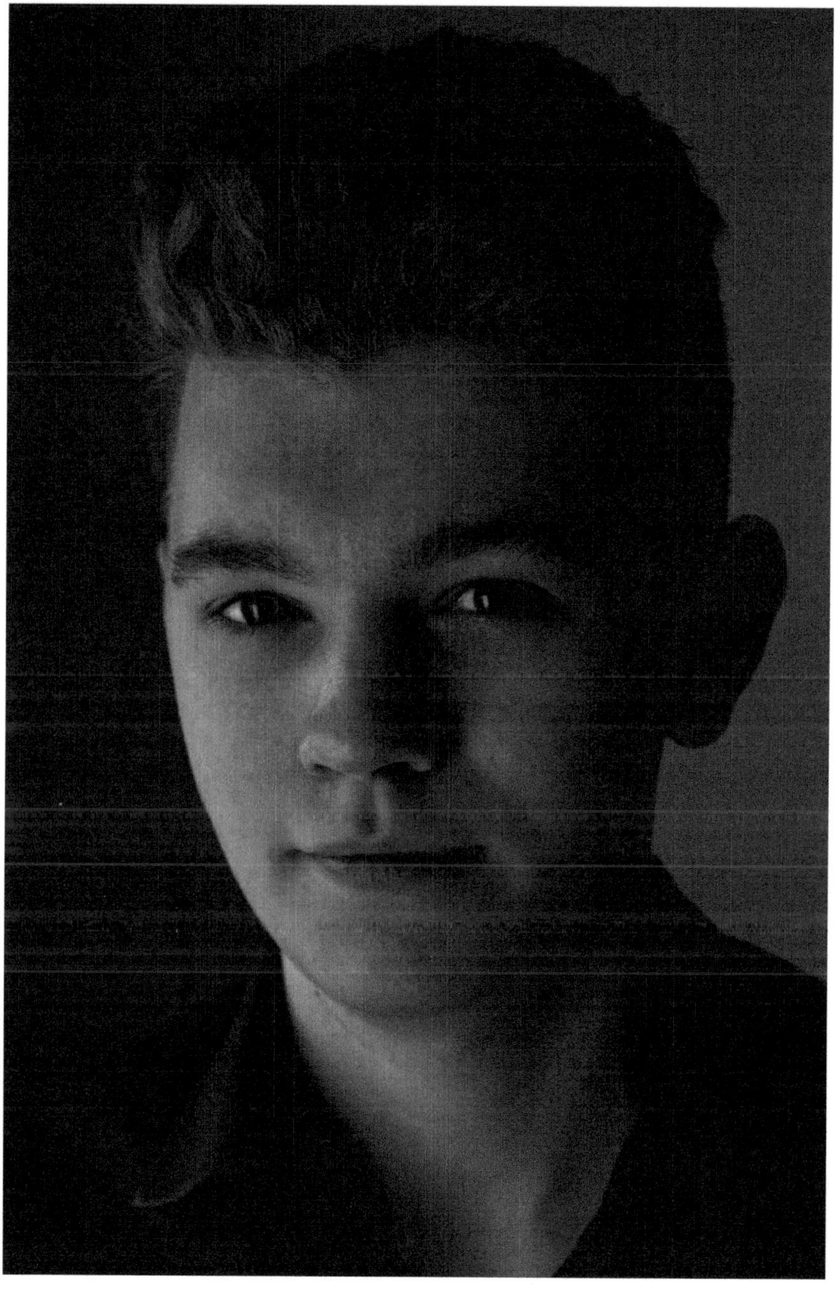

“This November there seems to be nothing to say”

Anne Sexton

HIDDEN POEM

Sometime in the future
I will know all I am
Just through a glimmer in your eye
And through nightly reminders, that I am still alive

Sometime in the future
The heart shall be free
And whilst, I shall not glare at the sky
The sun shall look down on me

Sometime in the future
The pain in my arms and legs shall cease
And be replaced by the delicate touch
Of you, and summer breeze.
You, and summer breeze.